MW00617422

The Count of Monte Cristo

LEVEL THREE   **1000 HEADWORDS**

OXFORD
UNIVERSITY PRESS

Great Clarendon Street, Oxford OX2 6DP

Oxford University Press is a department of the University of Oxford. It furthers the University's objective of excellence in research, scholarship, and education by publishing worldwide in

Oxford New York

Auckland Cape Town Dar es Salaam Hong Kong Karachi Kuala Lumpur Madrid Melbourne Mexico City Nairobi New Delhi Shanghai Taipei Toronto

With offices in

Argentina Austria Brazil Chile Czech Republic France Greece Guatemala Hungary Italy Japan Poland Portugal Singapore South Korea Switzerland Thailand Turkey Ukraine Vietnam

OXFORD and OXFORD ENGLISH are registered trade marks of Oxford University Press in the UK and in certain other countries

This edition © Oxford University Press 2010

The moral rights of the author have been asserted

Database right Oxford University Press (maker)

First published in Dominoes 2004

2014

20 19

ISBN: 978 0 19 424819 8 BOOK
ISBN: 978 0 19 424777 1 BOOK AND MULTIROM PACK
MULTIROM NOT AVAILABLE SEPARATELY

No unauthorized photocopying

Printed in China

This book is printed on paper from certified and well-managed sources.

ACKNOWLEDGEMENTS

The publisher would like to thank the following for permission to reproduce photographs: The film stills that appear in this book are courtesy of GMT Productions, 'Le Comte de Monte Cristo', un film realisé par José Dayan. Avec: Gérard Depardieu – Ornella Mutti – Jean Rochefort – Pierre Arditi – Sergio Rubini – Michel Aumont – Guillaume Depardieu – Jean-Marc Thibault. Scénario, adaptation et dialogues de Didier Decoin, d'après l'œuvre d'Alexandre Dumas. Un coproduction: TF1 – GMT Productions – DD Productions – Cité Films Productions – Mediaset SpA – Taurus Film. Diffusé avec le soutien du Programme MEDIA de l'Union Européenne. Avec la participation du Centre National de la Cinématographie. Producteur Associé: Jacques Bar. Produit par: Jean-Pierre Guérin. © 1998 – TF1 – GMT Productions – DD Productions – Cité Films Productions – Mediaset SpA. Stills courtesy of Second Line/Corbis.

Bridgeman Art Library Ltd pp (Napoleon (in Fontainebleau, 1846 (oil on canvas) by H.P.Delaroche/ Hamburger Kunsthalle, Hamburg, Germany), 24 (Still Life of Pipe Tobacco and Matches/William Harnett/Private Collection/Photo © Bonhams, London, UK); Christie's Images Ltd. p31 (pistol four barrelled flintlock 1782); Corbis pp13 (Château d'If/Parrot Pascal/Corbis Sygma), 24 (Sailor at the wheel/The Mariners' Museum), 24 (Cave/Joel W. Rogers), 74 (Alcatraz/Gerald French), 78 (Château d'If/ Parrot Pascal/Corbis Sygma); Getty Images pp6 (Marseille, France/Jacobs Stock Photography), 24 (Jewellery/Tony Hutchings), 25 (Ibex/John Giustina), 55 (Stone wall/ James Wells), 65 (Treasure chest/Nick Vedros & Assoc.), 70 (Waves breaking/Taxi); Kobal Collection p74 (Clint Eastwood in Escape From Alcatraz/Paramount/Malpaso); Magnum Photos p25 (Customs Officers/Chris Steele-Perkins); Mary Evans Picture Library p25 (Pirates bury stolen loot); OUP p19 (Shackles/Ingram); TopFoto p75 (Donington Hall/Topham Picturepoint).

Cover: iStockphoto (tall ship at sunset/Jason van der Valk)

DOMINOES

Series Editors: Bill Bowler and Sue Parminter

The Count of Monte Cristo

Alexandre Dumas

Text adaptation by Clare West

Alexandre Dumas was born near Paris in 1802. His grandmother was a Haitian slave, and his father, a general in the French army, died when Alexandre was only four. As a child, Dumas was poor, and had little education, but when he was twenty he went to live in Paris and soon became successful both as a playwright and a novelist. His most famous books, *The Three Musketeers* (1844) and *The Count of Monte Cristo* (1845) are both available in the Dominoes series. Alexandre Dumas died in 1870. His son, also called Alexandre, was a successful novelist, too.

OXFORD
UNIVERSITY PRESS

BEFORE READING

1 Napoleon is an important person in the story *The Count of Monte Cristo*. Complete this information about him with the words in the box. Use a dictionary to help you.

Napoleon Bonaparte was born in 1769 in Corsica. He agreed with the French Revolution of 1789, and the **(a)** .... of King Louis XVI.

In 1804 Napoleon became **(b)** .... of France and by 1807 France had a large Empire in Europe. But then Napoleon became unpopular. In 1812 he sent his **(c)** .... into Russia, where the hard winter killed many of his soldiers. In 1814 he lost the **(d)** .... of Leipzig and was sent away to the island of Elba in the Mediterranean.

After that, the **(e)** .... in France made Louis XVI's brother, Louis XVIII, the new king of France. (Louis XVI's son, Louis XVII, had died as a boy in prison.)

Early in 1815 Napoleon **(f)** .... from Elba and returned to France. The French army welcomed him as the Emperor of France and Louis XVIII left Paris.

Later Napoleon lost the battle of Waterloo. He was **(g)** .... to the island of Saint Helena in the south Atlantic and Louis XVIII returned to Paris. Napoleon died on Saint Helena six years later.

army
banished
battle
Emperor
escaped
execution
royalists

2 This story begins in 1815. Do these people from the story support the King, or Napoleon, or both? Write your answer.

a Monsieur Villefort, the crown prosecutor ....

b Renée Saint-Méran, the daughter of a rich, old family ....

c Monsieur Noirtier, an old soldier ....

1

A wicked plan

On February 24th 1815, a ship called the *Pharaon* sailed into Marseille, the largest **port** in the south of France. People ran to the waterside to welcome it, because the arrival of a ship is always a great excitement in Marseille, especially if it belongs to an owner from the town. A young man was standing on the **deck**, watching the sails and giving careful orders to the sailors. He was between eighteen and twenty years old, tall, with fine dark eyes and fair hair. His calm face showed that danger meant nothing to him.

The ship's owner, **Monsieur** Morrel, could not wait for the ship to arrive in port, and jumped into a small boat. 'Take me to the *Pharaon*!' he ordered his men, and soon he was on the ship's deck.

'Welcome home, Dantès!' he said to the young man. 'But where is Captain Leclère?'

'It's very sad, Monsieur,' replied Edmond Dantès, taking off his hat. 'We lost our good captain between Naples and Rome.'

'And the **cargo**?' asked the owner worriedly.

> **port** a town with a harbour, where ships can come in to land
>
> **deck** the floor of a ship
>
> **Monsieur** /mə'sjɜː/ the French word for 'Mr'
>
> **cargo** the things that a ship carries

The Pharaon *sailed into Marseille.*

1

'It's all safe, Monsieur. But poor Captain Leclère died very suddenly, after a short illness. We gave him a sailor's **funeral**, and there he rests, on the Mediterranean seabed.'

'Well, we all have to die at some time. As long as the cargo—'

'All is well with it, Monsieur. But here is Monsieur Danglars, who takes care of that side of things. You can ask him.'

The owner turned to a man of about twenty-five, with a dark, unsmiling face. The sailors hated him as much as they loved Dantès.

'Well, Monsieur,' said Danglars. 'You've heard the bad news.'

'Yes, yes, poor Captain Leclère. A fine, honest man.'

'And an excellent sailor, just the kind of man for an important company like Morrel and Son,' answered Danglars.

'Yes, although it's good to see that Dantès can take the captain's place so well,' said Morrel, watching Edmond.

'Well,' said Danglars, looking at Dantès with **hatred** in his eyes, 'he's young and **confident**. But he made us lose a day and a half by stopping at the island of Elba, for no good reason.'

'Did he?' replied Morrel, surprised. 'That was wrong of him. Dantès!' he called. 'Come over here! I'd like a word with you.'

The young man came closer. 'Yes, Monsieur?' he asked.

'I wanted to ask why you stopped at the island of Elba.'

'Monsieur, I had to obey Captain Leclère's last order. As he lay dying, he told me to take a letter to the **Emperor** Napoleon, who's living on Elba, and that's what I did.'

'Young man,' said Morrel, 'you did well to obey your captain, but perhaps you'll get into trouble for it. The King and his friends will be angry if they hear you've taken a letter to their worst enemy.'

'I only obeyed an order. Is that all, Monsieur?'

'I think the Emperor gave him a letter to take to someone in Paris,' Danglars whispered in the shipowner's ear. 'I – I saw it!'

funeral the time when a dead person is put under the ground

hatred a feeling of great dislike

confident sure of yourself

emperor king of a big country or a group of countries

'If Dantès has a letter, he'll tell me about it,' replied Morrel confidently. 'Dantès, you're free to go now. Can you come and have dinner at my house this evening?'

'Thank you for your kind invitation, Monsieur, but the first thing I must do is visit my father. He's an old man now.'

'You're a good son, Dantès. And you have another person to visit perhaps? A lover? The beautiful Mercedes?'

'We are not lovers, Monsieur,' the young man replied seriously. 'She is my **fiancée**. We hope to marry very soon.'

'Well, go now, Dantès, and in three months' time, come back to see me. The *Pharaon* will be ready for the next trip,' and Morrel put his hand on Edmond's shoulder, 'with its new captain.'

'Oh Monsieur!' cried Edmond in **delight**. 'Thank you a thousand times! It's my dearest wish!'

And with this wonderful news in his head, the young man walked quickly away from the waterside and into the narrow streets of the old town. Soon he came to a small house and hurried up the dark stairs to his father's room. Here he spent several hours with his father, making sure that the old man had everything that he needed. Then Edmond hurried out of Marseille, towards a fishing village.

꧁꧂

Mercedes, a lovely young girl with dark hair and beautiful soft eyes, was standing in her living room, looking dreamily out of the window at the sea. She was thinking of Edmond. Behind her a tall young man was speaking to her.

fiancée the woman that a man has promised to marry

delight a feeling of great happiness

Mercedes was thinking of Edmond.

3

'Please, Mercedes,' he was saying, 'think about our wedding! You know how much I love you! Give me your answer!'

'You've had it a hundred times, Fernand,' the girl replied. 'I love you like a brother, but my heart belongs to another man.'

'But I've dreamed of being your husband for ten years, Mercedes! Don't take away that hope! Say 'yes' to me!'

'Fernand, I love Edmond Dantès! I will marry no other man!'

'Perhaps he'll die! Or perhaps he's forgotten you!'

'Mercedes!' cried a happy voice outside. 'Mercedes!'

'Ah!' cried the girl, running to the door in delight. 'You see, he hasn't forgotten me! Edmond, I'm here!'

Suddenly, Edmond and Mercedes were in each other's arms. At first, their happiness cut them off from the rest of the world, and they saw nothing of what was around them. But then Edmond noticed Fernand, who had a dangerous-looking knife in his left hand.

'Who is this?' Edmond asked Mercedes.

'He will be your best friend, Edmond, because he's my very dear **cousin**. This is Fernand.'

Edmond smiled and put out his hand, but Fernand, his face dark and full of hatred, did not move. Mercedes stepped forward.

'Fernand, put that knife away, and remember this,' she said, her eyes shining angrily. 'If anything happens to Edmond, I shall kill myself. Now you're going to shake hands with him like a friend.'

Slowly Fernand offered his right hand, but as soon as Edmond touched it, he ran out of the house.

'What can I do, what can I do?' Fernand cried wildly.

'Stop a minute!' called Danglars, who was sitting under a tree with a bottle of **wine**. 'You look unhappy. Have a drink with me.'

Without really knowing what he was doing, Fernand sat down on the grass and drank the wine.

cousin the son or daughter of your uncle or aunt

wine a red or white alcoholic drink made from grapes

4

'So your lovely cousin Mercedes has decided, has she?' said Danglars. 'She's going to marry Edmond Dantès, is she?'

'Yes, and I can't stop it!' cried Fernand angrily.

'But you can if you want to, my friend,' said Danglars. 'Let me show you what to do. Just write a short letter to Monsieur Villefort, the **crown prosecutor**. In the letter you say that Dantès is an enemy of our King, because he's visited the **wicked** Napoleon on the island of Elba, and even carries a letter from him. You see? It's easy!'

'But if I do that, Edmond will die!'

'Who knows? Perhaps he'll go to prison. But what does it matter? You'll have the lovely Mercedes!' And to himself, Danglars was thinking, 'This will stop Dantès becoming captain of the *Pharaon*!'

Danglars' wicked plan worked well. The next day was Edmond's wedding day, but just as he and Mercedes were getting ready to go to the church, Edmond was arrested. Danglars smiled to himself as he watched the police take the young man away.

Edmond was arrested.

READING CHECK

Choose the best words to complete the sentences.

a On February 24th 1815 . . .

   1 ☐ Napoleon gives Edmond Dantès a letter.

   2 ☐ the captain of the *Pharaon* – Leclère – dies.

   3 ☑ the *Pharaon* arrives in Marseille.

b Dantès took a letter to Napoleon on Elba because . . .

   1 ☐ he had to follow Captain Leclère's orders.

   2 ☐ he is a friend of the old Emperor.

   3 ☐ he was paid for taking it.

c Monsieur Morrel wants Edmond to . . .

   1 ☐ be the next captain of the *Pharaon*.

   2 ☐ get into trouble.

   3 ☐ visit Mercedes.

d The first thing Edmond does in Marseille is to . . .

   1 ☐ go to Monsieur Morrel's house for dinner.

   2 ☐ visit his father.

   3 ☐ visit the beautiful Mercedes.

e When Edmond goes to visit Mercedes, she is . . .

   1 ☐ alone.

   2 ☐ angry with Edmond.

   3 ☐ with Fernand, who wants to marry her.

f Danglars doesn't want . . .

   1 ☐ Edmond to be the new captain of the *Pharaon*.

   2 ☐ Fernand to be unhappy.

   3 ☐ Mercedes to marry Edmond.

g Edmond is arrested because . . .

   1 ☐ Danglars wrote a letter to Villefort.

   2 ☐ Fernand wrote a letter to Villefort.

   3 ☐ Morrel wrote a letter to Villefort.

Marseille today

WORD WORK

1 Correct the boxed words in these sentences.

   a Beaujolais is the name of a famous French red **line** . ....wine........

   b Marseille is a **part** in the south of France. ....

   c Edmond Dantès is standing on the **neck** of the *Pharaon* when it arrives. ....

   d Danglars thinks of a very **picked** plan. ....

   e People in Europe often wear black to go to a **funnel** . ...

2 Find words in the knives to complete the sentences.

   a Napoleon was the E m p e r o r of France just before the story begins.   romerp

   b Mercedes is Edmond's f _ _ _ _ _ _ .   cinéea

   c Fernand is Mercedes' c _ _ _ _ _ .   nosiu

   d Villefort is the c _ _ _ _ p _ _ _ _ _ _ _ _ _ in Marseille.   worn tresuroco

   e Morrel is the owner of the *Pharaon* and its c _ _ _ _ .   gaor

   f Danglars is Edmond's enemy; he feels only h _ _ _ _ _ for him.   radte

   g Edmond is a very c _ _ _ _ _ _ _ _ young man.   fontiend

   h Mercedes cries with d _ _ _ _ _ _ when she sees Edmond.   thelig

GUESS WHAT

What do you think happens in the next chapter? Tick three boxes.

   a ☐ Villefort speaks to Edmond.   **d** ☐ Edmond goes to prison.

   b ☐ Villefort thinks that Edmond is a criminal.   **e** ☐ Mercedes marries Edmond.

   c ☐ Edmond can go free.   **f** ☐ Napoleon becomes Emperor again.

2

Another enemy

*M*onsieur Villefort was another man who was planning to marry his fiancée soon. As the crown prosecutor, he wanted a wife who would help him become an important person in Marseille. Now that Napoleon was **banished**, people who had helped him become Emperor, like Villefort's own father, were losing their jobs, homes, money and friends. Villefort hoped that no one would remember his father's interest in Napoleon, and he was clever enough to see that, from now on, only **allies** of the King would have **power** and make money. So he had chosen as his fiancée Renée Saint-Méran, who was beautiful and rich, and whose parents loved the King.

He was at a dinner party at their large house in the most expensive part of Marseille, when a letter was brought to him. He opened it at once and read it.

'Aha!' he said. 'This is serious. It seems there are still people who want to bring back the banished Emperor Napoleon!'

'Can that be possible?' said several people in **horror**.

'Yes. This letter tells me that a man called Edmond Dantès has visited the Emperor on Elba and has a letter for Napoleon's allies in Paris. The police have arrested him, and I must go to question him.'

'Poor young man!' cried Renée. 'Don't be too hard on him!'

'I must do what is necessary, dear Renée. But I'll return soon.' And Renée gave him her sweetest smile as he went out.

When he arrived at his office, he ordered the police to bring in their prisoner. As he questioned Dantès, he watched the young man's open, honest face and confident smile. 'He can't be a criminal!' he thought. 'Renée will be happy when she hears that I've **released** him!'

He smiled kindly at Dantès. 'You'll be free very soon, my

banish to punish someone by sending them away somewhere

ally a person that is on your side and helps you in a fight

power the feeling of being able to make other people do what you want

horror the feeling of being badly surprised and afraid

release to set free

friend,' he said. 'I'll just look at the letter that you were carrying.'

'Thank you, Monsieur! Here it is.'

Villefort looked down at the **envelope**, and went white with horror. It was addressed to Monsieur Noirtier, his father! He fell back in his chair.

'Monsieur, are you ill?' cried Dantès.

'I'm asking the questions, not you,' said Villefort, trying to think fast. 'Does anyone else know of this letter? Anyone at all?'

'No, Monsieur! But – what's the matter? Can I go now?'

'I'm afraid I must keep you a little longer. But first I'm going to destroy this letter. Then no one can say you're the King's enemy!' He threw the letter on the fire, where it burned brightly for a few seconds.

'Monsieur, you're a very good friend to me!'

Villefort looked down at the envelope.

'Now remember, Dantès, if anyone asks about that letter, say you know nothing about it. Don't forget – it's important!'

'I won't forget, Monsieur. Thank you!'

Villefort called a police officer to the room, and whispered an order to him. 'Follow this officer,' he told Dantès, who smiled gratefully at Villefort as he went out.

When he was alone, Villefort put his head in his shaking hands. 'The letter is gone now but Dantès read the name and address on the envelope. If anyone learns that my father is still one of Napoleon's allies, I'll lose my job at once!' he thought. 'They could even put me to death! But perhaps nobody will find out now.'

Dantès was taken to a police **cell**, where he waited for several hours. Then, to his great surprise, he was taken to the port by four large policemen carrying guns. They pushed him into a small boat, which they started **rowing** out to sea.

'What's happening?' asked Dantès. 'Monsieur Villefort promised he would release me!'

'We don't know anything about that,' said one of the men. 'We're just obeying our orders.'

'But where are you taking me? Tell me!'

'Haven't you guessed? Look around you!'

Dantès lifted his eyes, and suddenly saw a frightening black shape right in front of the boat. It was the **Château** d'If, a castle on a small rocky island, and it was well known to everybody in Marseille as a prison. No prisoner ever left it alive. He cried out in horror, 'My **God**! The Château d'If! Why are we going there?'

The policemen just smiled, and continued rowing.

'But that's a prison for the worst criminals, enemies of France! You can't take me there! I've done nothing wrong!'

Just then the boat touched the rock, and the policemen carried Dantès, who was fighting and shouting wildly, into the castle. Soon he found himself alone in a dark, silent underground cell.

cell a small room in a prison or police station

row to move a boat through water using long pieces of wood with flat ends

château /ʃæˈtəʊ/ the French word for 'castle'

God an important being who never dies, and who decides what happens in the world

He could not understand what had happened, and he felt that he was going **mad**.

As Villefort was returning to the Saint-Mérans' dinner party, he was stopped in the street by a beautiful dark-haired girl.

'Please tell me where Edmond Dantès is, Monsieur,' she said, her voice breaking with sadness.

'I can't tell you that – he's a criminal,' replied Villefort coldly, pushing Mercedes to one side. For a moment he felt worried about Dantès – to keep himself safe he had sent an honest young man to prison for life and destroyed any hope of happiness for Edmond and his fiancée. He knew that he had the power to put matters right. But the moment passed, and he did nothing.

The next day, Villefort travelled to Paris to tell the King that Napoleon was planning to escape from Elba. He hoped the King would ·be grateful for this information and **reward** him richly, but he was unlucky. While he was at the palace, news of the Emperor's escape was brought to the King, and the King was too busy worrying about his own future to think about rewarding the crown prosecutor.

In the next two weeks, many Frenchmen hurried to join Napoleon's army as it moved northwards, and finally the King had to leave Paris for a safer country. Napoleon became Emperor again.

Now Villefort had to be careful if he wanted to keep his job – people knew that he had spoken against the Emperor. Renée Saint-Méran was no longer the right wife for him and his plans for a wedding were soon forgotten. And when Monsieur Morrel, the owner of the *Pharaon*, asked him repeatedly about Dantès, he always pretended to be warmly interested in Edmond, but, sadly, unable to help. He hoped that no one would ever find out about the terrible thing that he had done.

mad crazy

reward to give money to someone for their help

11

READING CHECK

Put these sentences in the correct order. Number them 1–9.

a ☐ Morrel comes many times to ask Villefort about Edmond.

b ☐ Villefort sees that Edmond is a good man and decides that he can go free.

c ☐ Villefort is at a dinner party with the family of his fiancée.

d ☐ Villefort quickly burns the letter.

e ☐ Villefort goes to question Edmond about a letter from Napoleon.

f ☐ Villefort sees that the letter from Napoleon is to his father.

g ☐ Villefort secretly sends Edmond to prison.

h ☐ Napoleon becomes Emperor again and Villefort decides not to marry.

i ☐ Mercedes comes to ask Villefort about Edmond.

WORD WORK

Use words from Chapter 2 in the correct form to complete the sentences.

a The English and Germans were ...*allies*...... fighting against the French at the Battle of Waterloo.

b At the beginning of the story Napoleon was .... on the island of Elba.

c Villefort sees his father's name on the .... of a letter from Napoleon.

d Villefort's face goes white with .... when he thinks of the danger that he is in.

e Villefort decides that he cannot .... Dantès.

f Villefort has the .... to send men to the Château d'If.

g Some policemen .... a small boat out to the island prison.

h Dantès must live in one of the small .... there.

i When Dantès arrives at the prison he nearly goes ....

j He calls out to .... to help him.

k Villefort hopes that the king will .... him for information about Napoleon's plan to return to France.

The Château d'If today

GUESS WHAT

What do you think happens in the next chapter? Match the people with the sentences.

Edmond

Danglars

Fernand

Villefort

Napoleon

a ... is sent away to the island of Saint Helena.

b ... stays in prison for many years.

c ... marries Renée de Saint-Méran.

d ... joins the French army.

e ... leaves Marseille and goes to live in Spain.

3

A friend in prison

On June 18th 1815, Napoleon lost the great battle of Waterloo, and in the end was sent back to prison and then banished to the island of Saint Helena, where he stayed until his death. The King returned to Paris. Villefort married Renée Saint-Méran, and, feeling perhaps that people in Marseille knew too much about him, he moved with his wife to Toulouse, another town in the south of France.

Danglars and Fernand, whose plan had put Edmond in prison, were afraid that he would come back to take his **revenge** one day, so they both left Marseille. Danglars went to live in Spain, and Fernand joined the French army.

Edmond's father died soon afterwards, and kind Monsieur Morrel paid for the funeral. Now Mercedes was all alone. She spent her days crying for the young man she loved so dearly, with no hope that she would ever see him again.

A year after the King's return to France, the prison **inspector** came to visit the Château d'If. The **governor** welcomed him to the prison, saying with a smile, 'I'm afraid the prisoners will all tell you the same thing – they're **innocent** and they want to be free! But we *have* got two interesting prisoners, one mad and one dangerous.'

'Well, I'd like to see them before the others,' said the inspector.

Taking two **guards** with them, they went down to the underground cells, in the darkest and coldest part of the prison.

'This is the dangerous one,' whispered the governor, as the guards unlocked the door of Edmond's cell.

The young man jumped up in delight when he realized an inspector was visiting him. 'At last, Monsieur!' he cried. 'Now you can help to get me out of here, because I'm innocent of any crime!'

revenge something that you do to hurt someone because they have hurt you

inspector a person whose job is to visit a place and check that all is well

governor a person whose job is to manage a prison

innocent having done nothing wrong

guard a person whose job is to watch prisoners and stop them from escaping

The inspector and the governor smiled at each other. 'What did I tell you?' whispered the governor.

'Leave it to me, young man,' said the inspector. 'I can't promise anything, but I'll see what I can do.'

As Dantès was thanking him gratefully, they left his cell.

'This is the mad one,' whispered the governor, as the guards opened another door. 'He's an old **priest**, who thinks he has some **treasure** hidden somewhere. He'll offer you money to help him find it!'

When they entered, they saw an old man sitting on the floor, who spoke to them at once. 'How lucky you've come!' he cried. 'I have something very important to tell you.'

'Here it comes,' whispered the governor to the inspector.

'There is a lot of treasure waiting for me in a secret place, and if you help me, I'm ready to give you a large part of it.'

'You know your prisoners well,' said the inspector to the governor. To the priest he said, 'I'm sorry, Father, I can't help you.'

'Well!' replied the priest angrily. 'If you don't want my treasure, then I shall keep it. Goodbye!' And he turned his back as the governor and the inspector left his cell.

For several weeks after this visit, Edmond lived in hope. Surely the inspector would help to set him free! But when nothing happened, and the weeks became months and years, he was more miserable than ever. He knew that he was innocent, but he feared he would have to stay alone in this dark cell for the rest of his life. And he was only nineteen!

priest a person who works for the church

treasure something expensive, for example gold, silver or valuable stones

'I have something very important to tell you.'

15

But one night, as he lay awake on his hard bed, he heard a noise in the wall next to him. He listened carefully. 'It's another prisoner, digging a **tunnel**!' he thought excitedly. Using pieces of a broken plate, he too began to dig. Suddenly a stone fell out of the wall, and a grey head appeared in the hole. It was the priest, Father Faria. He had dug a tunnel all the way from his own cell to Edmond's.

Now a much happier time for Edmond began. He could visit Father Faria when he liked, using the tunnel, and together they discussed all kinds of things. Over the years the priest taught Edmond everything he knew; all about plants and natural medicines, about languages and the way of life in different countries, and about famous writers from the past. Soon they loved each other like father and son. Sometimes the priest talked of his secret treasure, which he said was hidden on the island of Monte Cristo, but Edmond always replied, 'Your teaching is the only treasure I want, Father.'

Edmond had another reason to be grateful to the priest, because Father Faria, after listening intelligently to the story of Edmond's arrest, was able to explain why it had happened.

'You see, my friend, Danglars wanted your job as captain of the *Pharaon*, Fernand wanted to marry Mercedes, and Villefort – well, he just wanted to save his own skin! His father – Monsieur Noirtier – was one of Napoleon's close allies and he knew

tunnel a long hole that goes through or under something

16

that you'd seen the old man's name on the envelope that you brought with you from Elba. These three wicked men are your enemies – they are the ones who sent you to prison.'

'I'll take my revenge on them one day!' said Edmond angrily. 'They'll be sorry for what they did to me!'

Many years passed in this way. But then one day, the priest became very ill. Just before he died, he gave two yellowish pieces of paper to Edmond. 'These tell you how to find the treasure on the island of Monte Cristo,' he said. 'It's yours now, my boy. Find it and use it well, and remember me.' That night he died, with Edmond sitting sadly at his bedside.

The next morning, when the guards found the old man dead, they put him in a **sack**. Edmond, who was in the tunnel, heard one of them say with a laugh, 'We'll take him to the **graveyard** tonight.'

Suddenly Edmond thought of a way of escaping. When they had gone, he took the body out of the sack and put it in his own bed in his cell. Then he returned to Father Faria's cell and lay down inside the sack on the old man's bed. He waited there all day.

That night the guards returned. They picked up the sack, which was surprisingly heavy for a thin old man, and carried it outside. Edmond could hear them laughing, as they tied something to his feet. He could smell the salt in the air and hear the sea crash against the rocks. Perhaps the guards would start digging soon.

But then they picked him up, one at his head and one at his feet. 'One! Two! Three!' they counted, and let go of the sack. Edmond suddenly found himself flying through the air, pulled downwards by the heaviness at his feet. With a crash he fell into frighteningly icy water, which closed around him. The guards had thrown him over the castle walls, with large stones tied to his feet – the sea was the graveyard of the Château d'If.

sack a large strong bag

graveyard a place where dead people are put under the ground

17

READING CHECK

Match the first and second parts of these sentences.

a When the King returns to Paris . . .

b Danglars and Fernand . . .

c When Edmond's father dies . . .

d Mercedes is alone and thinks that . . .

e The governor of the Château d'If thinks that Edmond . . .

f He says that Father Faria . . .

g Father Faria digs a tunnel . . .

h Edmond tells Father Faria . . .

i When Father Faria dies . . .

1 leave Marseille.

2 Edmond will never come back.

3 is a dangerous prisoner.

4 Edmond finds a way to escape from prison.

5 is mad because he talks about being very rich.

6 about his arrest and Father Faria explains why it happened.

7 Villefort finally marries Renée Saint-Méran.

8 to Edmond's cell, and they become friends.

9 Monsieur Morrel pays for the funeral.

WORD WORK

Match the words on the prison wall with the underlined words in the sentences.

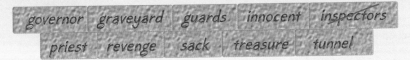

governor graveyard guards innocent inspectors
priest revenge sack treasure tunnel

a One day, one of the king's <u>men who visit to see that all is well</u> comes to the prison.
   inspectors

b He and the <u>man who tells the prison workers what to do</u> visit the prisoners.
   . . . .

c It is terrible when a man is <u>doing nothing wrong</u> and he goes to prison.
   . . . .

d Father Faria is a <u>man of the church</u>. . . . .

e Edmond and Faria secretly go to each other's cells through a <u>long hole in the ground</u>.
   . . . .

f Father Faria often talks about some <u>gold, silver and valuable stones</u> that he knows about. ....

g In the evening, the <u>men who watch the prisoners</u> come to take Faria's dead body. ....

h Edmond escapes from prison in a <u>large bag</u>. ....

i At the Château d'If, the sea is the <u>place where dead bodies go</u>. ....

j Thinking about his enemies, Edmond decides that he wants to have <u>a time when he hurts those who have hurt him</u>. ....

GUESS WHAT

What do you think happens in the next chapter? Tick the boxes.

a Edmond swims to . . .
   1 ☐ Marseille.
   2 ☐ the island of Monte Cristo.
   3 ☐ another island.

b The captain of a ship finds Edmond and . . .
   1 ☐ gives him a job as a sailor.
   2 ☐ kills him.
   3 ☐ takes him back to prison.

c Edmond . . .
   1 ☐ finds nothing on Monte Cristo.
   2 ☐ finds Father Faria's treasure.
   3 ☐ goes to Marseille with no money.

4

The island of Monte Cristo

*L*uckily Dantès was carrying a knife in his hand, and he managed to cut the sack open. But the stones tied to his feet were still pulling him downwards, so he searched for the rope and cut it. Then he swam powerfully upwards, and his head came up out of the water. He went down again at once, and swam under the water for fifty metres. When he came up again, he saw a black cloudy sky above the black stormy sea around him. Behind him, blacker than the sky or sea, stood the castle on its rock. And on the castle walls he could see the shapes of two men, looking down over the sea.

'Perhaps they've realized it wasn't a dead body that they threw over the walls!' Dantès thought. He swam underwater a long way, and when he came up again, he could not see the guards any more. He went on swimming in the darkness, and when his foot hit a rock, he realized he was on land. Although a strong wind was blowing and rain was falling, he was very tired and he fell asleep on the beach.

When he woke up, he realized he was on Tiboulen, a small island where no one lived. He noticed a small fishing boat in the water, near the rocks. He tried to warn the sailors, but clearly they could not **steer** their boat away from the danger. There was a terrible crash as their boat hit the rocks, and as Edmond watched in horror, four sailors fell into the water and were not seen again.

Little by little the wind died away and the sea became calm. Blue sky appeared between the clouds, and it was morning.

'Soon the guards will know that I've escaped!' thought Dantès. 'Then the police and **customs officers** will search the coast and all the islands! Where can I hide? Oh God, help me!'

Just then he saw a small ship coming towards Tiboulen.

steer to move a boat left or right

customs officer a person whose job is to catch people who take things, like wine and cigarettes, into a country secretly

'They're probably **smugglers**,' he thought. 'I'll pretend to be one of the sailors from the fishing boat, then I'll be safe with them for a while.'

He jumped into the sea and swam powerfully towards the ship. The captain saw him in the water, and ordered his men to help Edmond into the ship. They gave him food, water and dry clothes.

'Where do you come from?' asked the captain.

'I'm a Maltese sailor,' replied Dantès in Italian. 'Our boat broke up in the storm last night. My poor friends are all dead.'

'Do you know the coast and the ports round here?'

'Yes, I've been sailing these seas all my life.'

'Well, perhaps you'd like to stay with us and work for me on this ship. I need someone like you.'

Just then, they heard a loud bang from the Château d'If.

'What's going on there?' cried the captain.

'A prisoner probably escaped last night,' said Dantès, smiling. 'That's the warning gun.' The captain looked quickly at Dantès, but the young man seemed very calm, and the captain did not think he could possibly be the escaped prisoner.

'I'd like to work with you, captain,' continued Dantès. 'By the way, what's the date – the year?'

'You don't know what year it is?'

'I was so frightened by last night's storm – I nearly went mad!' replied Dantès, laughing. 'I've almost forgotten my own name!'

'Well, today's date is February 28th, 1829.'

Fourteen years before, to the day, the police had arrested Dantès. He had entered the Château d'If at nineteen and left it at thirty-three. Sadly he wondered what had become of Mercedes. Then, with the light of hatred in his eyes, he thought of the revenge that he would take on his enemies, Danglars, Fernand, and Villefort.

smuggler a person who takes things, like wine and cigarettes, into a country secretly

For the next three months he worked with the smugglers, helping them sail in and out of the ports along the coast, with a cargo of gold, **jewels**, **tobacco**, and other expensive things. They kept away from the customs officers, who often followed them and shot at them.

One day the captain said to Dantès, 'Well, my Maltese friend,' (Edmond had not told them his name, so that is what they called him) 'tomorrow we're taking on a cargo of silver and tobacco from another ship, at the island of Monte Cristo.'

Edmond tried to stay calm. 'How long will we stay there?' he asked. He hoped he would have time to search for the treasure.

'Only a few hours,' said the captain.

It was an exciting moment for Edmond when the ship arrived at Monte Cristo that evening. It was a hilly island, and its rocks were turning pink and then blue in the light of the dying sun. As the smugglers jumped on to the beach, Edmond took a gun, telling them he was going to shoot a wild **goat** for supper.

He managed to shoot a goat and gave it to the sailors to cook over a fire on the beach. But as he walked away, he seemed to catch his foot on a rock, and fell heavily, with a loud cry of pain. The sailors came running to help him. But he told them he was too badly hurt to walk; they would have to leave him on the island for the night, and return to pick him up the next day. They agreed, and in an hour's time, they sailed away with their new cargo.

As soon as they had gone, he jumped up and, on a flat stone near the fire, put together the two pieces of paper that the priest had given him.

jewel a valuable stone

tobacco dried leaves used for making cigarettes

goat an animal which lives in the mountains and can jump from rock to rock

cave a large hole in the side of a mountain

*You will find gold coins, jewels and silver in the **caves** on the island of Monte Cristo. Go eastwards from the beach in a straight line and up the hill. Lift the twentieth rock from the small tree.*

Taking a burning stick from the fire, he went up the hill and found the twentieth rock. Under it there was a large stone with a ring in it. Before he tried to lift it, he looked all around, but no one was watching. He pulled the ring as hard as he could, and very slowly the heavy stone moved, uncovering a hole in the ground. 'The caves!' he thought in delight. He climbed down into the hole and found himself in a kind of underground room, and there, in the darkest corner, was a large wooden box. He hurried to open it, and fell back when he saw what was inside. It was full of shining gold coins, bright jewels and valuable silver – it was indeed treasure!

The next morning he was ready, with his pockets full of gold, when the smugglers came to pick him up. He asked them to leave him at the port of Marseille. Here he bought a fast sailing boat and returned to the island, alone, to fetch the rest of his treasure. And when he sailed back to Marseille again, he was one of the richest men in the world.

It was indeed treasure.

READING CHECK

Correct eight more mistakes in the chapter summary.

Edmond ~~sails~~ *swims* to the island of Tiboulen. He sees a police boat hit the rocks and the four sailors on it die. Later a small ship comes towards Tiboulen and Edmond swims to it. The sailors on the ship help Edmond out of the sea and give him money, water and dry clothes. Edmond tells them he is from Malta. The captain gives him a job as a sailor. There is a warning gun from the Château d'If to say that a prisoner has died. Edmond learns from the ship's captain that he has been in prison for four years. After three years of working on the ship, Edmond arrives on the island of Tiboulen. He pretends to fall and says that he is too badly hurt to swim with the others. He stays on the island for the night, and, with Napoleon's papers to help him, he finds the old man's treasure. Edmond Dantès becomes a very rich man!

WORD WORK

Match the words with the correct pictures.

a ~~jewels~~
......*steer*......

b goat
....

c cave
....

d steer
....

e smugglers

f tobacco

g customs officers

....

....

....

GUESS WHAT

What do you think happens in the next chapter? Tick the boxes.

a ☐ Edmond ☐ Villefort finds that his father is dead.

b ☐ Fernand ☐ Danglars has made lots of money as a banker.

c ☐ Fernand ☐ Danglars has become famous as a French army officer.

d Mercedes has married ☐ Fernand ☐ Danglars and now has a son.

e Edmond helps Monsieur Morrel by ☐ lending him money. ☐ being the captain of the *Pharaon*.

5

An English gentleman

antès bought himself an English passport in the name of **Lord** Wilmore. He dressed in expensive clothes, and put on a grey **wig**. When he saw himself in a mirror, he knew that nobody would recognize him.

He went immediately to the house where his father had lived, but it was empty. So he bought it for 25,000 **francs**. That evening, he visited a fishing village near Marseille. He stayed for an hour at a poor sailor's house, asking for news of several people who had disappeared about fourteen years earlier. The next day, the man got a new fishing boat – a present from Lord Wilmore.

Now Edmond had found out what he wanted to know. His poor father had died soon after hearing that his son was in prison, still confident that Edmond was innocent. Villefort, Danglars and Fernand were all now living in Paris. Danglars had made a lot of money as a banker in Madrid, and was now a **baron**. Fernand had also done well as an army officer in France and Greece; he was now a rich **gentleman**, and called himself Monsieur de Morcerf. Mercedes had waited over a year for Edmond to return, and then, miserable and lonely, she had agreed to marry Fernand; she was now **Madame** de Morcerf, with a son called Albert. It was painful for Edmond to think of her in Fernand's arms.

Lord Wilmore's next visit was to an important banker in Marseille. 'Monsieur,' he explained, 'I work for the Thomson and French company in Rome. Morrel and Son of Marseille **owe** us 100,000 francs, and we've heard they're in serious difficulties.'

The banker was glad to help. 'I think the best person to give you information is Monsieur Boville, the prison inspector. Morrel owes him money, too. He lives opposite the church.'

lord an important man, from a good English family

wig false hair

franc money that was used in France

baron an important man, from a good French family

gentleman a man from a good, usually rich, family

Madame /mə'dɑːm/ the French word for 'Mrs'

owe to have to pay back money that you have borrowed from someone

When Lord Wilmore arrived at Boville's house, he recognized the inspector as the man who had visited him in his cell in the Château d'If. But his English **disguise** worked well and the inspector did not recognize him at all.

'Ah, monsieur!' said Boville, when he was asked about Morrel and Son. 'You're right to be worried! Morrel owes me 200,000 francs, and if the *Pharaon* does not return in a week's time, he'll be unable to pay me back!'

'I'll pay the **debt** for Morrel,' offered the Englishman. 'My company doesn't like bad debts.'

There was a look of delight on Boville's face, as Lord Wilmore paid him. 'Is there anything I can do for you, Monsieur?'

'Just tell me – you're the prison inspector, I understand – I used to know an old priest in Rome, who died in the Château d'If.'

'Oh yes, Father Faria! He was mad. Poor man!'

'Was there a young man in the prison at the same time?'

'Yes, Edmond Dantès – he died while trying to escape.'

'I see. Thank you, Monsieur.'

The next day Lord Wilmore went to see Morrel. He found the ship-owner at his desk, looking grey and old.

disguise
something that you wear so people cannot recognize you

debt the money that you owe

Lord Wilmore went to see Morrel.

'Monsieur, I come from the Thomson and French company. I'd like to inform you that I've paid off some of your debts.'

'How – how much do I owe your company?' asked Morrel, white-faced. He had no idea that he was in fact talking to his old friend Edmond Dantès.

'300,000 francs. I don't think you'll be able to repay me,' said Wilmore.

'No, Monsieur, I haven't got the money—'

Just then a beautiful sixteen-year-old girl ran in, crying, 'Father! Bad news! The *Pharaon* is lost!'

Morrel looked at her in horror. 'And the captain, Julie? The men? Are they all safe?'

'Yes, all safe, but the ship was **wrecked** in a storm and the cargo is lost!'

Morrel put his head in his hands. 'Thank God the men are safe! But I'm **ruined**!'

The Englishman stepped forward. 'Let me give you three months to find the money, Monsieur,' he said. 'I'll be back here at 11 o'clock on September 5th, for you to pay me what you owe me.'

'You're very kind, Monsieur,' said Morrel.

On his way out, the stranger met Julie on the stairs, and said to her, 'You'll get a message from someone called Sinbad the Sailor. Do what the message tells you. Promise me.'

'I promise, Monsieur,' said Julie, wonderingly.

ᢗᡒᡭᢍ

The three months passed, and Morrel had found no way of paying the Englishman. His wife had written to their son Maximilien, asking him to come home from the army for a few days, because she was so worried about her husband. On September 5th, Morrel ate no breakfast and went to sit in his office alone. Julie feared the worst – she knew her father kept a gun in his desk.

When Maximilien arrived, he went to see his father.

wrecked of a ship, broken at sea by a storm or by crashing onto rocks

ruined of a businessman, with no more money

'Father, what has happened?' he asked.

'You're an honest man, my son, so you'll understand. I owe money that I can never repay. I cannot go on living!'

'Father, let me die with you!'

'Then who will take care of your mother and sister? Promise me that you will not kill yourself!'

'I promise, Father.' He put his arms round his father to say goodbye, and then ran out of the room.

Morrel, alone again, looked at the clock. Two minutes to eleven. He picked up his gun and put it

Morrell sat in his office alone.

to his head. Just then Julie ran in, waving a red **purse** and some papers.

'Father! Stop!' she cried. 'I got a message from someone called Sinbad the Sailor, asking me to fetch this purse from his house. And inside, look! Here are your debts, all paid! You owe nothing!'

Suddenly they heard shouting outside in the street. 'The *Pharaon*! The *Pharaon* is arriving!' Morrel and Julie ran out of the house and down to the port, where they found a large crowd, all watching a beautiful new ship sailing in. On her decks were the men from the old *Pharaon*, and on her side was her name in bright newly-painted letters.

'But I don't understand. I thought the *Pharaon* was wrecked. This is wonderful!' said Morrel, crying openly.

A tall man wearing a grey wig smiled as he watched from behind a building. 'Be happy, Morrel,' he whispered, unheard. 'Now I've repaid you for your goodness in the past.'

purse a small bag, like a wallet, to keep money in

READING CHECK

Match the sentences with the people.

1 Danglars   **2** Monsieur Morrel   **3** Lord Wilmore

4 Monsieur Boville *(the prison inspector)*   **5** Fernand   **6** Sinbad the Sailor

a 3 . is Edmond in the disguise of a rich Englishman.

b . . . is now Monsieur de Morcerf and is married to Mercedes.

c . . . has made lots of money in Madrid.

d . . . talks to Lord Wilmore about money that Morrel must pay him.

e Lord Wilmore gives . . . the money that Morrel should pay him.

f Lord Wilmore visits . . . and asks him for money.

g His ship the *Pharaon* is lost at sea and . . . can't pay Lord Wilmore.

h Lord Wilmore speaks to Morrel's daughter, Julie, about . . . .

i Three months later Julie brings money from . . .
  to help her father.

BARON DEBT GENTLEMAN LORD
OWE PURSE RUINED WRECKED

WORD WORK

Match the words from the gun with the correct definition.

a ....lord........ an important man from an English family

b .... an important man from a French family

c .... when a ship is broken on rocks

d .... when a businessman has no more money and his business is finished

e .... a bag for putting money in

f .... money that you must pay to someone

g .... to have to give money that you borrowed back to someone

h .... a man from a good family

GUESS WHAT

In the next chapter we meet the Count of Monte Cristo. Tick three boxes.

a ☐ The Count of Monte Cristo is Edmond's new disguise.

b ☐ The count meets Sinbad the Sailor.

c ☐ The count is friendly with criminals.

d ☐ The count marries Mercedes de Morcerf.

e ☐ The count takes his revenge on Baron Danglars.

f ☐ The count saves Albert de Morcerf's life.

g ☐ The count loses all his money.

Sinbad the Sailor

In early 1838, two young men who lived in Paris, Monsieur Albert de Morcerf and his friend Baron Franz d'Epinay, decided to spend that year's **carnival** in Rome. Before the start of the carnival, Franz travelled to Livorno because he had heard of an island near there that was a good place to shoot wild goats. It was not difficult to find a small boat and pay the captain to take him to this island, which was called Monte Cristo.

But when they arrived at the island, they saw there was already a group of men on the beach, sitting round a fire.

'Smugglers, **Excellency**,' said the captain. 'Or **bandits**. They can be dangerous.'

In fact he was welcomed by the men on the beach, and he was even invited to have dinner with their chief. They tied an old shirt over his eyes, so he could not see anything, and took him into a deep cave. When they uncovered his eyes, he looked round in delight. It was like an underground palace, with thick carpets and rich wall-hangings.

The chief was a good-looking man, with bright, intelligent eyes, black hair and beard, and very white skin. 'Welcome to my home,' he said in French to Franz. 'You can call me Sinbad the Sailor. My **servants** will get you anything you want.'

For Franz, it was like being in a dream. He spent the evening in pleasant conversation with the man who called himself Sinbad, drinking wine and eating some of the best food he had ever tasted. He fell asleep on one of the thick carpets.

When he woke up next morning, he found he was lying just outside the cave. He went to join the captain and sailors of his boat, who were having breakfast on the beach.

'**Signor** Sinbad had to leave early,' explained the captain.

carnival a time when many people come together in the streets to dance, sing, and wear fantastic clothes

Excellency a very polite way of talking to someone important

bandit a robber who attacks travellers

servant a person who works for someone rich

Signor /sɪnˈjɔːr/ the Italian word for 'Mr'

'See the white sail over there? That's his ship. He's on his way to Malaga.'

'But from the way he's sailing he's going to Corsica, not Malaga!' said Franz.

'Ah!' said the captain, smiling. 'He's got two friends with him – bandits, you could call them – so he's taking them there first.'

'Bandits? Isn't Sinbad afraid that the police will catch him?'

'Not him!' laughed the captain. 'His ship's faster than any police boat.'

Franz no longer had any interest in shooting goats. He decided to return to Livorno, leaving the mysterious island behind him.

⁕

The next day Franz arrived in Rome and met Albert at their hotel. They asked the hotel-owner, Signor Pastrini, to find them a **carriage**, but he explained he only had a very old one to offer them.

'But remember, Excellencies,' he warned them, 'don't drive outside the **city** walls at night! There are bandits!'

'Franz, this is exciting!' said Albert. 'An adventure, at last!'

'Be serious, Excellencies. Luigi Vampa is the bandits' chief. He **kidnaps** people and sometimes kills them!' explained Signor Pastrini.

They drove off, to see the Colosseum in the moonlight. Albert sat dreaming on a stone seat, while Franz walked a little further away. As he stood in the shadow of a wall, he realized that he could hear two men on the other side of the wall, having a secret conversation.

'What have you discovered, Luigi?' asked one. To his surprise Franz recognized the voice of Sinbad the Sailor.

'There'll be two **executions** on Tuesday, Excellency, and one of the men to die is my poor friend Peppino.'

'Don't worry. I'll make sure he gets a **pardon**.'

carriage an old kind of car that horses pull

city (*plural* **cities**) a big and important town

kidnap to take someone away as your prisoner

execution when someone is punished for a crime by being killed

pardon when someone decides not to punish someone for a crime

'If you can save him, Excellency, I'll do anything for you.'
And the two men disappeared into the shadows.

After Franz and Albert had returned to the hotel and gone to bed, Franz spent a sleepless night, wondering what kind of man Sinbad the Sailor was – rich, powerful, and friendly with bandits.

The next evening Franz and Albert went to the theatre. As they were young men with a greater interest in women than in the actors, they spent most of their time looking round at the other theatre-goers. Suddenly Franz saw a beautiful young woman in Greek clothes, and next to her was the man he knew as Sinbad! There was something hard about the line of his mouth that made Franz **shudder**. The young man promised himself he would find out more about Sinbad.

When he and Albert returned to the hotel, Signor Pastrini came to their room with a message. 'The **Count** of Monte Cristo is staying here in the hotel, Excellencies, and has heard that you gentlemen need a better carriage. So he's offering you seats in his carriage, and places at the windows of another hotel. You can watch the carnival from there. He also invites you to visit him tomorrow morning.'

So the next morning the two young men were shown into the count's rooms by a richly-dressed servant.

When the Count of Monte Cristo came in, Franz saw through his disguise and recognized him at once as Sinbad the Sailor, but he said nothing. He and Albert found many interesting things to discuss with the count, and soon they started talking about the next day's executions.

'It's terrible to think of putting two men to death, in cold blood,' said Franz. 'Were the poor men's crimes really so bad?'

'Listen,' said the count, his eyes suddenly full of hatred, 'if a man hurts or murders your father, mother, or lover, is prison enough? Is even execution enough? Isn't revenge much, much sweeter?'

shudder to shake because you are afraid, or because you think someone or something is unpleasant

count a man who is more important than a lord or a baron

'Surely,' said Franz, 'if you take revenge, the police will arrest you and you'll have to pay, perhaps with your life.'

'Not if you're rich, powerful, and intelligent! But gentlemen, why are we talking about this at carnival time? I see my servants have got lunch ready. Why don't you join me?'

Albert found many interesting things to discuss with the count.

During the excellent lunch, Franz tried to discover what Albert thought of the count. But his friend was too interested in the count's food and conversation to worry about anything else. Franz noticed that the count was also looking closely at Albert, and he could not understand why.

༺༝༝༺

In the afternoon, all three went in the count's carriage to watch the executions from the windows of the Hotel Rospoli. A large crowd filled the square, as the two prisoners were brought to the foot of the **guillotine**. At the last moment a soldier ran up waving a piece of paper. Peppino was free to go, and the guillotine fell on only one prisoner that day.

The next day Franz and Albert lost themselves in the excitement of carnival. The count had kindly lent them his carriage. So, wearing **masks**, they drove up and down the streets

guillotine a machine that was used at that time in France to execute people (by cutting off their heads)

mask a cover that you put over your face to hide it

of Rome, waving and throwing flowers to any pretty girls in the other carriages. Albert felt sure that a beautiful woman in a green mask was interested in him, and when he got a note from her, he read it out excitedly to Franz.

'Tomorrow at seven o'clock, get out of your carriage at the church of San Giacomo and meet me on the steps.'

And the following evening, Franz watched Albert meet the lady at the church, and go off into the crowd, arm in arm with her.

But later that night Franz began to worry about his friend. Rome could be a dangerous city during carnival, especially at night.

Suddenly there was a knock on his door, and Signor Pastrini brought in a man with a letter in his hand. Franz thought that he recognized Peppino, but he was more interested in the letter. It said:

> *Franz, bandits have kidnapped me. Give all the money in my travelling bag to the man who brings you this note.*
> *Albert*

And under this message, it said in Italian:

> *If I don't have 20,000 francs in my hands by 6 o'clock in the morning, Monsieur Albert will die.*
> *Luigi Vampa*

Franz read the note in horror. He knew that he and Albert did not have 20,000 francs. Suddenly he had an idea, and went along to the count's rooms. The count listened with interest to Franz's story.

'Don't you think,' said Franz, 'that if we go together to meet Luigi Vampa, he'll let Albert go free?'

'But what power have I got over this bandit?'

'Didn't you save Peppino's life two days ago? And isn't Luigi Vampa very grateful to you?'

The count wondered how Franz knew about that, but he agreed to help. He, Franz and Peppino drove beyond the city walls, and then Peppino took them through a number of underground caves and tunnels to where the bandits were. Their chief, Luigi Vampa, was surprised to see the count, and very angry with his men when he realized that Albert was a friend of the count's. He refused to take any money from Franz.

So Albert was a free man again, and when they arrived back at the hotel, he said, 'You saved my life, Count. I'm very grateful!' He held out his hand, and Franz noticed the count shudder as he shook it. 'I hope, one day, I'll see you in Paris, Count, where my parents will be able to thank you themselves.'

'I have some business there in three months' time,' said the count. 'May I visit you then? Say, 21st May? At half past ten in the morning? I'm leaving Rome tomorrow, so goodbye for now, my friends.'

Luigi Vampa was surprised.

READING CHECK

Tick the boxes to complete the sentences.

a ☐ The Count of Monte Cristo
☑ Franz d'Epinay visits Italy with Albert de Morcerf to see the carnival.

b ☐ Albert
☐ Franz meets Sinbad the Sailor on the island of Monte Cristo.

c Back in Rome, Franz hears ☐ the count ☐ Luigi Vampa talking secretly with Sinbad.

d The next evening Franz sees ☐ the count ☐ Luigi Vampa at the theatre.

e Franz notices that the count is very interested in ☐ Albert. ☐ Peppino.

f ☐ Albert
☐ The count disappears with a woman during carnival.

g Albert sends a note to ☐ Franz ☐ the count asking him for money.

h Franz goes with the count to speak to ☐ Peppino. ☐ Luigi Vampa.

i Luigi Vampa lets Albert go free when he realizes that he is a friend of ☐ Franz's. ☐ the count's.

WORD WORK

Find words in the masks to complete the sentences.

a Albert and Franz want to visit Italy during c <u>arnival</u> time.

b Sinbad the Sailor's s _ _ _ _ _ _ _ look after Franz on the island of Monte Cristo.

c Albert and Franz go to see the e _ _ _ _ _ _ _ _ of two criminals one day.

d At the last minute one of the criminals gets a p _ _ _ _ _ and can go free.

e Signor Pastrini tells Franz and Albert not to go outside the c _ _ _ walls late at night.

f Franz s _ _ _ _ _ _ _ _ when he looks carefully at Sinbad in the theatre.

g The Count of Monte Cristo says Albert and Franz can travel in his c _ _ _ _ _ _ _ _ .

h Albert and Franz wear m _ _ _ _ _ to go to the carnival.

i Luigi Vampa is a well-known b _ _ _ _ _ _ in Rome.

j Luigi Vampa k _ _ _ _ _ _ Albert.

GUESS WHAT

What do you think happens in the next chapter? Write *Yes* or *No*.

a The Count meets Albert's family in Paris. ......

b Baron Danglars becomes the Count's banker. ......

c The Count tries to kill Villefort. ......

d The Count meets and falls in love with Julie. ......

The count in Paris

*T*hree months later, in the house in Paris where Albert and his parents lived, everything was ready for the Count of Monte Cristo's visit. At ten o'clock in the morning Albert's friends started arriving – Monsieur Lucien Debray, Monsieur Beauchamp, Baron Château-Renaud, and Maximilien Morrel, who was wearing his army officer's uniform.

Half an hour later, a servant threw open the door of Albert's dining room and said, 'His Excellency the Count of Monte Cristo!' All the young men turned to look at the count, who entered, dressed in the most **elegant** clothes. He came forward, smiling, and was introduced to Albert's friends. When he heard the name of Morrel, his eyes shone and he shook Maximilien's hand, saying, 'Monsieur is clearly a brave soldier!'

This surprised everyone, but Château-Renaud said, 'You're right, Count. He saved my life in the last battle that we were in.'

'I was there at the right time, that's all,' said Maximilien.

'Talking of saving lives,' said Albert, 'it was the count who saved mine when I was in Rome for the carnival with Franz d'Epinay.'

'Come, come, Albert!' laughed Debray. 'You'll tell us you were kidnapped by bandits next!'

'Debray, you've guessed it!' said Albert. 'Now please sit down, and I'll tell you all the story of a dangerous bandit called Luigi Vampa and a poor Frenchman called Albert de Morcerf.'

The story **impressed** all Albert's friends, and they turned once more to look at the count with even greater interest. But he clearly wanted to talk about something else: 'Did I hear,' he asked, turning to Albert, 'that you are planning to marry very soon?'

elegant expensive and fashionable

impress to stay in your thoughts because it is interesting

'Well, Count, it's true that my father wants me to marry Baron Danglars' daughter Eugénie,' replied Albert.

'She'll bring two million francs with her!' said Beauchamp.

'Baron Danglars?' said the count. 'Ah, yes, I have **letters of credit** for him – he'll be my banker while I'm in Paris.'

The conversation moved on, and an hour or so later, Albert's friends said goodbye and left the house. Albert took the count to his parents' sitting room, and sent a servant to find them. Monsieur de Morcerf was the first to arrive. Fernand did not recognize the count, who kept his face half hidden.

'Welcome to my house!' de Morcerf said. 'I shall always be grateful to you for saving the life of my only son.'

Before the count could reply, another door opened, and a woman entered. 'Here is my mother!' Albert said.

Albert's friends were impressed by the count.

letter of credit
a letter asking a banker to give money to someone; another bank will pay back the money to the banker later

Monte Cristo, turning quickly, saw Madame de Morcerf standing in the doorway. Mercedes shuddered as the count stood up and **bowed** deeply. She bowed too, in silence. Had she seen through his disguise?

'Are you ill, mother?' asked Albert, hurrying towards her.

'No,' she said, smiling. 'I was just thinking how much I owe to this gentleman.' She moved towards the count, walking like a queen. 'Let me thank you, Count, with all a mother's feeling. Albert is safe and well because you helped him when he was in danger.'

She went on to invite the count to spend the rest of the day at their house, but he politely refused, and left soon afterwards.

Later, when Albert found his mother alone, they started talking about their guest.

'Does he really have the **title** of 'count'?' asked Mercedes.

'Yes, mother. He owns an island called Monte Cristo, and the title comes with it.'

'How old do you think he is?' she asked.

'Between thirty-five and thirty-six, I suppose.'

'So young? It's impossible!' Mercedes whispered. She shuddered. 'Albert, be very careful. Is this man really your friend?'

'I think so, mother. I like him. And he saved my life!'

His mother did not reply to this, and their conversation ended.

❧

The count's **steward**, Bertuccio, had found an elegant house in an expensive part of Paris for Monte Cristo to live in. There was also a house in **Auteuil**, a village just outside Paris, which

bow to put down your head in front of someone important

title a word like Lord, Baron or Count that you add to your name because you are important

steward a personal servant

Auteuil /əʊˈtɔɪ/

42

the count was interested in. So Bertuccio had bought it for him. That evening the count ordered Bertuccio to go with him to see the house in Auteuil. But as they were coming closer to the house, the count noticed how worried Bertuccio seemed to be. And when they entered the house, the steward could not hide his feelings, and cried out, 'Excellency, something terrible happened here! This was Monsieur Villefort's house, you see—'

'The crown prosecutor, who married Renée Saint-Méran?'

'Yes, he's a wicked criminal, and the crime happened here!'

'Bertuccio, tell me all about it.'

And there in the moonlight, the steward told his story:

'In 1815 my brother was murdered, but when Villefort refused to punish the murderers, I promised that I would take revenge on him. In the next few years I followed Villefort secretly, and discovered that, although he was married to Renée Saint-Méran, the crown prosecutor was keeping a **mistress** in a house in Auteuil. That was this house which now belongs to you, Excellency.'

The count smiled and Bertuccio went on.

'One night I hid in the garden, hoping to kill Villefort. Suddenly the crown prosecutor hurried out of the house with a small wooden box in his hands, and dug a hole in the ground, where he hid the box. At that moment I jumped out from behind a tree and pushed a knife deep into the prosecutor's chest. I did not wait to see if he was dead, but took the box out of the hole and ran out of the garden.'

'Go on, Bertuccio,' said the count, his eyes shining with interest.

'Well, when I heard a cry come from the box, I opened it and found a new-born baby boy inside. I took the baby to one of the city's **orphanages**. But a few

mistress a married man's lover

orphanage a home for children whose parents are dead

Bertuccio told his story.

years later, I and my dead brother's wife, Assunta, decided to take care of the boy ourselves, so we went to fetch him from the orphanage. We called him Benedetto and made him one of the family. Sadly, he was naturally wicked, and one night, when he was fourteen, he stole all our money while I was away from home, set fire to the house and ran away. And poor Assunta was found dead the next morning.'

When Bertuccio finished speaking, the count said kindly, 'No one will punish you for what you've done. You didn't kill Villefort, and he'll pay for his crimes, don't worry. We will return to Paris now.'

Since his arrival, the ladies and gentlemen of Paris could talk about nothing except the count. He sent Bertuccio to buy Madame Danglars' horses at twice their price, and then gave them back to her as a present. Then he sent his letters of credit to Baron Danglars, so the banker had to give him 500,000 francs at once, and worry about finding another five million by the end of the year. With his houses, servants, carriages and horses, the Count of Monte Cristo lived more elegantly and expensively than anyone else in Paris.

The count found out that Maximilien Morrel had left Marseille after the death of his father. He now lived with his sister Julie and her husband Emmanuel, in a pleasant house in a quiet part of Paris. He went to visit them, and realized at once how much these three people loved each other. In their sitting room he noticed a small red purse on a table, and asked Maximilien about it.

The young man picked up the purse and **kissed** it. 'This purse, Count, was touched by the hand of a man who saved our father from death – a stranger who called himself Sinbad the Sailor.'

'I haven't yet lost hope,' said Julie, 'that one day I may find him and kiss his hand.' She was looking closely at the count. Did she recognize something of Lord Wilmore in him?

kiss to touch lovingly with your mouth

'I do know an Englishman, called Lord Wilmore,' said the count, hurriedly turning his face away from her, 'who has very often helped people.'

'Oh Monsieur, if you cannot bring him to us, tell us where he is! We'll show him how deeply grateful we are to him!'

The count had **tears** in his eyes as he turned back to her and watched her lovely face carefully. 'Madame, I fear Lord Wilmore may no longer be alive.'

'Oh Monsieur!' whispered Julie, tears running down her face.

'Dear sister,' said Maximilien, 'remember what our good father often told us – it was not an Englishman who saved him.'

The count shuddered. 'Your father said what, Monsieur?'

'My father thought the man was someone who had come back from the dead – a dear, dear friend whom he had lost. When he was about to die, his last words were, "It was Edmond Dantès."'

For a moment the count could not say a word. Then he picked up his hat and said to Julie, 'Madame, I'm grateful to you for the peace that I find here – it's the first time for many years that I've been able to forget my troubles.' And he hurried away down the street.

'He's a strange man, this count,' said Emmanuel.

'Yes,' replied Maximilien, 'but he has a good heart.'

'His voice touched me deeply,' said Julie, 'and two or three times I thought it wasn't the first time I'd heard it.'

tear the water that comes from your eye when you cry

Maximilien repeats his father's dying words.

READING CHECK

What do they say?
Complete the sentences.

1 Baron Danglars will be my banker.

2 His voice touched me deeply.

3 I shall always be grateful to you for saving the life of my only son.

Is this man really your friend?

4

5 Let me thank you, Count, with all a mother's feeling.

My father wants me to marry Baron Danglars' daughter. **6**

7 This purse was touched by the hand of a man who saved our father from death.

8 This was Monsieur Villefort's house.

a 'My father wants me to marry Baron Danglars' daughter.' .... says Albert.

b ....
.... answers the Count of Monte Cristo.

c ....
.... says Fernand de Morcerf to the count.

d ....
.... says Mercedes to the Count.

e ....
.... Mercedes asks Albert.

f ....
.... Bertuccio tells the count.

g ....
.... Maximilien tells the count.

h ....
.... says Julie about the count.

WORD WORK

Use words from Chapter 7 in the correct form to complete the Count of Monte Cristo's diary.

I arrived in Paris with **(a)** .....letters of credit.... for Baron Danglars and went to visit Albert at once in my most **(b)** .... clothes. Albert's story of my meeting with Luigi Vampa **(c)** .... his friends. Then Albert's parents thanked me. Mercedes **(d)** .... when she met me but I wonder if she really believes my **(e)** .... of Count. A week or two later Bertuccio, my **(f)** .... bought a house for me in Auteuil. But when we went to see it, Bertuccio told me that it had been Villefort's house in the past and that the crown prosecutor had met his **(g)** .... there. He told me that in secret, in that same house, this woman had Villefort's son - a boy who later went into an **(h)** .... Not long after this I visited Maximilien Morrel and his sister, Julie. Maximilien **(i)** .... Sinbad the Sailor's red purse in front of me and told me how the money from it had once saved his father. Maximilien.told me that his father's last words were 'It was Edmond Dantès'.

GUESS WHAT

What do you think happens in the next chapter? Tick the boxes.　　　　**Yes　No**

a　The Count of Monte Cristo marries Villefort's daughter.　　□　□

b　The Count of Monte Cristo goes to the theatre with Fernand de Morcerf.　　□　□

c　Benedetto, Villefort's lost son, returns in disguise.　　□　□

d　The Count invites the Villeforts and the Danglars to his house in Auteuil.　　□　□

⁓ 8 ⁓

Love and money

*M*onsieur Villefort's wife, Renée Saint-Méran, had died young, leaving him a daughter, Valentine. He married again, and, with his second wife, had a son, Edouard. They all lived in Villefort's large house in Paris, with his father, Monsieur Noirtier, who was **paralysed** after an illness. Valentine loved her grandfather dearly, and she spent many hours taking care of him.

Valentine loved her grandfather.

Behind the house was a large flower garden, and then a high stone wall. On the other side of the wall were fields, where poor people grew their vegetables. One evening that spring, a young man disguised in workman's clothes walked up to the wall. He took a stone away from the wall and called softly through the hole, 'Valentine!'

'I'm here, Maximilien!' replied a girl in a white dress, running through the garden to the hole on her side of the wall.

'Do you still love me?' asked the young man.

'You know I do, Maximilien. But what can I do? My **stepmother** hates me because I have more money than her son, and my father wants me to marry Baron Franz d'Epinay!'

'Valentine, I'll die before I see you married to another man! We'll have to run away together and have a secret wedding!'

'I think you're right— Oh, go away! Someone's coming!'

Maximilien left the wall and quickly started digging. He heard a servant saying to Valentine, 'Your stepmother is asking for you, **Mademoiselle**. The Count of Monte Cristo has arrived.'

At that moment the count was in Madame Villefort's sitting

paralysed unable to move your arms or legs

stepmother the wife of your father but who is not your mother

Mademoiselle /ˌmædmwəˈzel/ the French word for 'Miss'

room. He had come, he said at the door, as a new neighbour to visit the family. But he really wanted to learn more about Villefort's home life as part of his plan to take revenge on the crown prosecutor. So he talked about anything and everything, and Madame Villefort, who loved the sound of her own voice, sat and talked openly and freely with him. He had already discovered that she had no time to take care of the paralysed Monsieur Noirtier, that she loved her little son more than anyone else, and that she thought Valentine's money should belong to Edouard. Now they were talking about **poisons**, which greatly interested the prosecutor's wife. When Valentine entered, Madame Villefort introduced her to the count and then sent her away a few minutes later. She closed the door carefully after the girl.

'Now, Count, let's continue our conversation,' she said. 'You were telling me how a person can **protect** himself against poison.'

'It's easy, Madame. You take a few drops of the poison every day, a little more each time. Then after a month you and another person could drink poison from the same glass. The person who had drunk it with you would die, while you'd just feel a little unwell.'

'How interesting!'

'I've studied medicines and poisons during my travels round the world. I've made a most useful medicine – one drop makes you feel fresh and alive, but five or six would kill you. And you can't taste it!'

'I wonder – could you possibly let me have some? I so often feel tired – I'm sure it would help me.'

The count promised to send the medicine to her the next day, and left the house, delighted with a successful visit.

⋘⋙

That evening, Albert and his friend Château-Renaud went to the theatre. They saw Madame Danglars, sitting with her lover

poison something that kills people when they eat or drink it

protect to save someone from danger or something unpleasant

49

Lucien Debray and her daughter Eugénie.

'Eugénie's a beautiful girl,' said Château-Renaud.

'I'd prefer someone gentler,' said Albert. 'But, look at the **box** over there!'

All eyes in the theatre were turned towards the box. A man in black, between thirty-five and forty years old, had just entered with a beautiful young woman in a long white dress, covered with jewels.

'It's Monte Cristo and his Greek **slave**, Haydée!' said Albert.

'A slave?!' repeated Château-Renaud.

'That's what he calls her. I think he bought her, somewhere in the East, to protect her from some terrible danger.'

Just then Albert's father came into the theatre. When Haydée saw Fernand de Morcerf, she gave a little scream.

'My lord,' she whispered to the count, 'who is that man?'

'Monsieur de Morcerf, who fought in Greece under your famous father, and was well paid for it, I understand.'

'It was this man who sold my poor father, Ali Pasha, to the enemy! We thought he was our friend, but when the enemy offered him money, he helped them to kill my father! I hate him!'

'Come, child, you're getting too excited. We'll go home.'

Albert, Château-Renaud, and the other people in the theatre could not hear this conversation. They thought the Greek girl was unwell, as they watched the count taking her out of the box.

⋯✥⋯

The next day, a young man in Italian clothes was shown into the count's sitting room.

'Ah, it's Andrea Cavalcanti, isn't it?' said the count, remembering the new name and the false life story that he had given to Villefort's son Benedetto.

'Er – yes, Count,' replied the young man, trying to remember what he had learnt. 'I come from a good old Italian family.

box an expensive seat in a small room at the theatre

slave a person who must work for no money

When I was a child, I was – er – kidnapped by bandits, so it's some years since I last saw my – er – dear old father. Your friend Sinbad the Sailor seemed to think you could help me.'

'Of course, my dear Cavalcanti,' said the count. The young man clearly had no idea that Monte Cristo and Sinbad were one and the same man. Then the count called to his servant, 'Bring in **Major** Bartolomeo Cavalcanti at once!'

An old man in uniform entered. 'Excellency, is this the man who – I mean, is this my son?' he asked the count, trying to forget his criminal past and remember his new name and life story, too. 'Lord Wilmore told me I'd find him here.'

'That's right, Major,' smiled the count. The old man clearly hadn't seen through his different disguises either. 'And now that you've found each other again, let me give you some money to help you live for a while in this expensive city. I think 50,000 francs each will do to start with.'

The young man and the old man looked at each other, their mouths open. It was more money than they had ever dreamed of.

'On Saturday I'd like to introduce you to some of my friends,' the count went on. 'So come to my house in Auteuil at five o'clock.'

After they had left, the count sent an unsigned message to Lucien Debray, saying that he should sell any Spanish **bonds** that he owned, because the Queen of Spain was in danger from her enemy Don Carlos. He knew what would happen – at once Debray told Madame Danglars, who told her husband. Danglars sold all his Spanish bonds. But the next day he realized the news was not true. He had lost a million francs.

The count's plans for revenge were going well.

꒷꒰꒦꒱꒷

At five o'clock on Saturday, carriages began to arrive at the count's house in Auteuil. First came Baron Danglars and his wife, with Lucien Debray and Maximilien Morrel, and then

major an officer in the army

bond money put into a company which is protected by the government

Villefort and his wife. The count smiled secretly as he noticed that both Villefort and Madame Danglars looked around fearfully as they entered the house.

Just then he found Bertuccio at his shoulder. 'Excellency,' said the steward, 'The woman over there—'

'You mean Madame Danglars?'

'I don't know her name. But that's her, the woman who was Villefort's mistress and lived in this house! And, my God!' He turned white as he saw Andrea Cavalcanti, 'Benedetto!' he whispered.

'Stay silent and go back to your work,' said the count.

After dinner, the count offered to show his guests round the house. Danglars chose to stay downstairs, talking about business with the Cavalcantis; he liked them because he felt sure they were very rich.

'I must show you one of the bedrooms,' said the count.

'I think someone **committed** a crime there. Follow me!' And he took the rest of his guests into a small dark bedroom on the first floor. 'You see? It's painted red. Think of the blood that surely fell here!'

Villefort looked white, and Madame Danglars fell into a chair.

'And here are some secret stairs that go down to the garden!' cried the count, throwing open a small door. 'I feel sure that the criminal

*'Be strong!'
said Villefort
to Madame
Danglars.*

went this way, taking a dead body out of the house, to hide it in the garden!'

'I need some air!' cried Madame Danglars.

'And in fact,' continued the count, 'I *know* a crime was committed, because when my men were digging in the garden, they found a box with a dead baby's body in it!'

'That's serious,' said Debray. And as the guests left the room and went downstairs, Villefort took the chance to whisper in Madame Danglars' ear, 'The count knows our secret. I'll find out what he's planning. Be strong! Say nothing to anyone!'

Villefort did indeed try to find out more about the count, but in the next few days his own family began to give him more to worry about. Madame Saint-Méran, Villefort's old **mother-in-law**, came to stay at the Villeforts' house. She wanted to see her granddaughter Valentine married as soon as possible, so the **signing** of the **contract** to marry Franz d'Epinay was fixed for nine o'clock in the evening of that same day.

Maximilien was wild with worry that he would lose his Valentine, and they agreed they would run away together that evening. But he waited and waited at the hole in the wall, and Valentine did not come. Later he discovered that her grandmother had died suddenly, and that the doctor thought she had died from poison. The person who would get all her money was Valentine, and no one else seemed to have any reason to poison the old lady. Behind closed doors people began to say that perhaps Valentine was a poisoner, and the servants began to leave the Villeforts' house one by one.

Maximilien was now very unhappy.

Maximilien was now very unhappy. He did not believe all the stories, but he knew that his plans to marry Valentine would have to wait. He was ready to kill Franz d'Epinay if necessary, to protect Valentine from a husband whom she did not love.

mother-in-law the mother of your wife or husband

sign to write your name

contract the paper that everyone signs to show that they all agree to something

READING CHECK

Complete these sentences with the correct names.

> Andrea Cavalcanti   ~~Maximilien Morrel~~
>
> Baron Danglars   the Count of Monte Cristo
>
> Edouard Villefort   Fernand de Morcerf
>
> Madame Danglars   Madame Villefort   Valentine Villefort

a Valentine loves .Maximilien.Morrel..........

b Madame Villefort hates ....

c She thinks Valentine's money should belong to ....

d The count says that he will send some medicine to ....

e Albert sees .... at the theatre with a Greek woman called Haydée.

f .... sold Haydée's father to the enemy.

g .... loses a million francs when he sells lots of bonds.

h Bertuccio recognizes .... as Villefort's mistress.

i Bertuccio knows that .... is Villefort's lost son, Benedetto.

j People think that .... killed Madame Saint-Méran for her money.

WORD WORK

Find the words in the wall on page 55 to complete the sentences.

a Villefort looks after his father, Monsieur Noirtier, who is ...paralysed...

b Madame Villefort is Valentine's ....

c Madame Villefort talks about .... with the Count of Monte Cristo.

d The count calls Haydée his 'Greek ....'.

e The count and Haydée sit in a .... at the theatre.

f Baron Danglars sells all his Spanish ....

g .... Cavalcanti says that he is Andrea's father.

h The Count of Monte Cristo wants to show the people visiting his house in Auteuil that someone .... a crime there.

i Madame Saint-Méran, Villefort's ...., wants to see the .... of her granddaughter's wedding contract.

j Maximilien Morrel wants to .... Valentine from marrying someone that she doesn't love.

GUESS WHAT

Match the first and second parts of these sentences to find out what happens in the next chapter.

a Villefort wants . . .

b Villefort's father wants . . .

c Albert doesn't want . . .

d Albert wants . . .

e Mercedes doesn't want . . .

1 to hear that his father helped to kill Haydée's father.

2 Baron d'Epinay to marry Valentine.

3 to speak to Franz.

4 the count to fight with Albert.

5 to fight the Count of Monte Cristo.

9

Revenge!

illefort was **determined** to marry his daughter Valentine to Franz d'Epinay, so he invited the young man home with him after Madame Saint-Méran's funeral, in order to sign the wedding contract. But when they were all in the sitting room, ready to sign, a servant hurried in, saying, 'Monsieur Noirtier wants to see Baron d'Epinay at once!'

Villefort, Franz and Valentine went up to the bedroom of the paralysed old man. He could only move his eyes, but over the years Valentine had learnt how to understand his wishes. He now made it clear to her that there was a paper in his desk, which he wanted Franz to read.

The young man read the paper aloud. Now, for the first time, he discovered what had happened to his own father, a **royalist**. In 1815, Monsieur Noirtier was with a group of men who wanted Napoleon to return to France. They had kidnapped Franz's father, because he was a royalist, and then Monsieur Noirtier himself had killed him! There were tears in Franz's eyes as he read the words.

The next day he wrote to Villefort, saying that he no longer felt able to marry Valentine. She was very grateful to her grandfather for stopping a wedding that she really did not want to happen.

At the same time, Baron Danglars, whose business was not doing well, was becoming more and more impressed with young Andrea Cavalcanti. 'It would be useful to have a lot more money in the family!' he thought. 'And now that I've heard about the terrible things that Albert's father did in the Greek war, I don't think that I want his son to marry my daughter. Not good for business!' So when Andrea asked the baron if he could marry Eugénie, Danglars was happy to agree.

determined
having decided to do something

royalist someone who loves and fights for their king or queen

The next day Albert was reading a newspaper when he noticed, to his horror, a short **article** which said:

'We have just discovered that, in the Greek war, a French officer took money from the enemy to help them kidnap and murder Ali Pasha, a friend of the French. The officer's first name was Fernand.'

Albert hurried round to the newspaper offices at once, to speak to his friend Beauchamp, who worked there.

'Beauchamp,' he cried. 'Look at this article! My father's first name is Fernand. Everyone will think that he did this terrible thing!'

'Don't worry, Albert. I'll find out if it's true.'

Three weeks later, Beauchamp visited Albert at home. 'Bad news, my friend,' he said. 'I've been to Greece, and I have these papers for you. They show that the article in the newspaper was true. Your father was indeed a **traitor**. I'm sorry.'

Albert looked at him with staring eyes.

'But as you're my friend,' said Beauchamp kindly, 'let me burn these papers now, and people will soon forget the story.'

They burnt the papers there and then.

But the story reappeared in other newspapers, and soon even the gentlemen of the **Upper House** were talking about it. When Monsieur de Morcerf arrived there one day, he found that everyone was looking angrily at him, and he was asked to explain what had happened between him and Ali Pasha in the Greek war. Silence fell as the Upper House waited for his answer. His face was white and his hands were shaking as he spoke.

'I'm no traitor, gentlemen,' he said. 'I was a friend of Ali Pasha, and I tried to save him, but I arrived too late.'

'No, traitor!' cried a woman's voice from the **public** seats. 'You're lying! You accepted the enemy's gold for the head of

article a piece of writing in a newspaper

traitor a person who goes against his allies or country

Upper House a group of important people, like lords, barons and counts, who meet to make laws for the country

public open to everyone; all the people

Ali Pasha! That's why you're rich today! I know, because I was there and saw it all! I am Haydée, Ali Pasha's daughter!'

All eyes turned to the public part of the House, where the Greek girl was standing. Then they looked back at Monsieur de Morcerf. He bowed his head and said nothing. The Upper House took only a few minutes to decide that he was a traitor, and should no longer sit in the House. De Morcerf went home alone.

'I am Haydée.'

Albert had heard from Beauchamp that it was Baron Danglars who had sent the information about his father's past to the newspaper. So he went to call on the banker.

'It wasn't my idea, young man,' explained Danglars. 'It came from the Count of Monte Cristo.'

'The count!' cried Albert in horror. 'But I thought he was my friend!'

He went straight to the theatre, where the count was in his usual box, with Maximilien Morrel.

'Count!' said Albert, throwing open the door of the box. 'You must give me an explanation!'

'I do not accept "must" from anyone,' said the count icily.

'But you will accept my invitation to fight, perhaps?'

'Shall we say tomorrow at ten in the morning?'

Albert bowed and left the box, and the count smiled.

But when Monte Cristo returned home that night, he found

a woman waiting to see him. It was Madame de Morcerf. Mercedes had not wanted to recognize Edmond openly in front of her husband, but it was clear now that she knew who the Count of Monte Cristo really was.

'Oh, Edmond!' she cried. 'Please do not kill my son!'

'I have promised to take my revenge, Madame, not on Albert, but on his father Fernand, who married my fiancée, as you know.'

'Oh Edmond! You should punish *me*! I wasn't strong enough to wait for you. I

'Please do not kill my son!'

thought you were dead. Edmond, I may not be as beautiful as I was, but I love you still! Don't let me see the man I love become the murderer of my son!'

'What is it that you want?' he asked. 'Your son's life? Well then, he shall live.'

Mercedes gave a cry that brought tears to his eyes. 'Oh Edmond! Thank you, thank you! You are so good!'

'But your poor Edmond won't live long. Tomorrow he must die, if Albert is to live,' replied the count.

Her beautiful eyes were wet with tears, as she offered him her hand. 'Don't say that, Edmond. There is always hope. God will not let you die.' And with that, she left the room.

The count sat there in the darkness, thinking miserably of his plans of revenge, which his promise to Albert's mother had destroyed. Now he seemed to have nothing left to live for.

But the next morning, at the meeting-place, he was surprised

'I'm sorry,' said Albert to the count.

to see Albert coming towards him in a friendly way.

'Monsieur,' said Albert as calmly as he could, 'I'd like to say I'm sorry, not because my father was a traitor to Ali Pasha, but because he was a traitor to you, his friend, when you were both young men in Marseille. My mother has told me everything. You were right to take revenge on my father, and I, his son, say so!'

Mercedes had bravely told Albert her painful secret, in order to keep both him and the count alive. With a tear in his eyes, the count shook hands warmly with Albert. There was no fight that day. Some of Albert's friends looked coldly at him the next time they met, and whispered that he had not been brave enough to fight the count.

When Fernand de Morcerf saw his son return home unhurt, he could not understand what had happened, and ordered his servant to drive him straight to the count's house. He was shown in at once.

'Count, my son had good reason to fight you today.'

'You think so, Monsieur?' replied the count coldly. 'In fact, he said he was sorry, so the fight didn't take place.'

'He said he was sorry? He didn't fight you?'

'No, he realized his father had committed terrible crimes.'

'Why do you say that? Who are you? What's your real name?'

'You know me very well. You married my fiancée, after all!'

Monsieur de Morcerf gave a cry of horror. 'Edmond Dantès!' With shaking legs he ran out of the room and returned home in the carriage. While Albert and Mercedes were packing their clothes and getting ready to leave the house that they both now hated, because they knew that it was paid for with a traitor's money, Fernand went to his bedroom. There he took a small gun from his desk, and as the carriage that was taking away his wife and son left the house, a shot rang out.

News of Monsieur de Morcerf's death had only just reached his neighbours, when they heard another piece of interesting news. Andrea Cavalcanti was supposed to sign the contract to marry Eugénie Danglars at nine that evening. But just as the banker was about to sign, the police entered the house and arrested Andrea. It appeared that he had escaped from prison and had since committed a murder. In the excitement, no one noticed Mademoiselle Eugénie quietly leave the house. She had decided to stay unmarried, and was going off to travel round Spain and Italy with a woman friend.

The count was pleased with the success of his plans so far. Fernand was dead, Danglars would soon be **bankrupt**, and there was a poisoner at work in Villefort's house. But when Maximilien, whom the count loved like a son, told him that Valentine was his fiancée, the count realized he could not let her die, along with the rest of Villefort's family. Maximilien felt sure someone was giving her poison, but the count promised the young man that he would protect her from danger.

That night the count visited Valentine in her room, by using some secret stairs that led from the house next door. He explained that it was her stepmother who was trying to poison her, and gave her a special **sleeping potion**, which would make her appear to be dead.

bankrupt having no money and a large debt

sleeping potion medicine that makes you go to sleep

The next morning, the servants found Valentine silent and cold in her bed. The doctor saw Madame Villefort with a glass of poison in her hand, and felt sure that she must be the murderer, so he told her husband. But poor Maximilien heard the news with horror – he had Monte Cristo's promise that Valentine would not die – and now he felt that his life had ended.

Villefort decided the funeral would be on the following day. That night the count, again using the secret stairs, visited Valentine's bedroom, where her body lay in its **coffin**. He had something important to do before that coffin left for the graveyard.

Valentine's body lay in its coffin.

The next day, Maximilien's sadness, as he watched his fiancée's coffin going into the ground, was great. But the count was watching him, and followed him back to his sister's house. Here he found the young man writing a letter, with his gun on the desk.

coffin a box that you put a dead person's body in

'My dear young friend, you mustn't kill yourself!'

'But the woman who meant everything to me is dead! Who are you to give me orders?'

'The man who saved your father! I am Edmond Dantès!'

Maximilien jumped up and called to his sister and her husband. They came running to throw themselves at the count's feet and kiss his hand. But the count knew that Maximilien was still thinking of death, so he asked them to leave him alone with Maximilien again.

'Keep your hope alive, my friend,' he said. 'Come and stay with me for a month. And if at the end of that time, you still want to kill yourself, I'll put a gun in your hands myself.' Maximilien agreed to this.

A week later, Andrea Cavalcanti appeared in **court** to answer for his crimes. But when the crown prosecutor asked what his real name was, the young man explained that he was Villefort's own son, left to die in a box in the Auteuil garden. To the horror of everyone in court, Villefort bowed his head and said it was all true. Then he left the court and hurried home.

There, in this house of death, he found the bodies of his wife and son, both poisoned by her hand. As he was looking at them, he heard a voice behind him say, 'Monsieur, you've finally paid your debt to me!'

He turned to find the Count of Monte Cristo standing there. 'What debt?' he asked.

'I am Edmond Dantès!' said the count.

'Well, Edmond Dantès, look!' screamed Villefort, showing him the two bodies. 'Have you had your revenge now?' He ran wildly out into the garden, and started digging. 'I'll find him soon!' he cried. 'The box must be here somewhere!'

'He's gone mad!' thought the count. 'Perhaps I've done too much! Enough is enough.'

court the place where people decide if someone is innocent of a crime or not

READING CHECK

Tick the boxes to complete these sentences.

a Franz d'Epinay doesn't want to marry Valentine after Monsieur Noirtier

- ☐ talks to him
- ☑ makes him read about his father's death.
- ☐ lies to him

b Albert learns from

- ☐ the Count of Monte Cristo
- ☐ Haydée that his father helped to kill
- ☐ the newspaper Ali Pasha.

c

- ☐ Haydée
- ☐ the Count of Monte Cristo tells everyone that Monsieur de Morcerf took gold
- ☐ Beauchamp for Ali Pasha's head.

d Albert decides he must fight

- ☐ Danglars.
- ☐ the count.
- ☐ Beauchamp.

e

- ☐ Mercedes
- ☐ Monsieur de Morcerf goes to see the count the night before the fight to stop it.
- ☐ Albert

f

- ☐ Fernand
- ☐ Albert kills himself when the fight doesn't happen.
- ☐ The Count of Monte Cristo

g

- ☐ Andrea Cavalcanti
- ☐ Maximilien Morrel wants to marry Eugénie Danglars.
- ☐ Beauchamp

h

- ☐ Andrea Cavalcanti
- ☐ Madame Villefort is arrested for murder.
- ☐ Valentine

i Cavalcanti explains to the crown prosecutor that he is

- ☐ Villefort's
- ☐ Mercedes' son.
- ☐ Major Cavalcanti's

WORD WORK

Find words in the treasure to complete the sentences.

a Villefort is determined. that Valentine should marry Franz d'Epinay.

b Franz comes from a .... family.

c Albert reads an .... about his father in the newspaper.

d The newspapers say that Fernand was a ....

e People in the .... ask questions about Monsieur de Morcerf's past.

f Haydée's voice comes from the .... seats and she tells her story.

g Baron Danglars loses all his money and will soon be ....

h Andrea Cavalcanti tells everyone in .... that Villefort is his father.

i The Count of Monte Cristo gives Valentine a .... to make her seem dead.

j Maximilien is sad when he sees Valentine's .... go into the ground.

GUESS WHAT

Who do you think is happy in the last chapter? Tick four boxes.

a ☐ Albert de Morcerf   **e** ☐ The Count of Monte Cristo

b ☐ Mercedes   **f** ☐ Baron Danglars

c ☐ Valentine   **g** ☐ Maximilien

d ☐ Haydée   **h** ☐ Luigi Vampa

10

A new life

*M*aximilien was still **depressed** after Valentine's funeral and couldn't stop thinking of taking his own life, so the count decided to take him to Marseille. When they arrived at the port, they saw that a large army ship was leaving for North Africa. The count watched a woman on the **dockside** who was waving goodbye to a man on the ship.

'Look, Count!' cried Maximilien, pointing at one of the passengers. 'It's Albert de Morcerf, in soldier's uniform!'

'Yes,' said the count. 'I know.'

When Maximilien said that he wanted to go alone to see his father's **grave**, Monte Cristo followed the woman from the dockside back to his father's old house. He had given Mercedes the house to live in.

He pushed open the door and found Mercedes in the garden.

'Oh, I'm so unhappy!' she said, with tears in her eyes. 'My son has left me to join the army!'

'He did well. He must work for your future and his.'

Mercedes sadly shook her head. 'There is no future for me, Count. I have drunk deeply from life's **bitter** cup. But here at least I can die where I was once so happy!'

The count **raised** her hand to his lips and kissed it sadly. 'What will you do now, Mercedes?'

'I'll stay here in your father's house, and **pray**. My life is finished. Say goodbye to me, Edmond!'

They held hands for a moment, and then Mercedes ran into the house. The count never saw her again.

While walking back to the port, an idea suddenly came to the count. 'Perhaps I should go to the Château d'If again, to **remind** myself of the horror of it!' So he asked the captain of a passing fishing boat to take him there.

depressed very sad all the time

dockside the place around a port, where the cargo is put on and taken off ships

grave a hole in the ground where you put a dead body

bitter very sad, not sweet

raise to lift up

pray to speak privately to God

remind to make somebody remember something

As the boat came close to the great black rock, he felt the same **terror** as on that first journey. But the castle was no longer a prison, and was now open to the public. The **caretaker** showed the count his own cell, and told him the story of the prisoner who was thrown into the sea in a sack. 'That was me!' thought Monte Cristo. 'How long ago it seems now!'

When he returned to Marseille, the count found Maximilien praying beside his father's grave. 'Maximilien,' he said, 'I have business in Rome, so I'll leave you here for two weeks. But on October 4th I'll send a boat to fetch you, and you'll come to meet me on the island of Monte Cristo.'

'Count, on October 5th it'll be a month—'

'I know. Wait and hope! Now, goodbye until then!'

Just before Valentine's funeral, the count had asked for his five million francs in gold coins from Baron Danglars. The baron had paid, but that meant he was now bankrupt. The following day Danglars had packed his bags and left Paris for ever, taking the count's letters of credit with him. When he arrived in Rome, he went at once to the bank that the letters came from, and asked them for the money that they owed him. To his delight, the count had not written to the bank to stop the money, and he was given the five million francs in gold coins with no trouble at all.

But on his way back to his hotel, he was kidnapped by Luigi Vampa's men and taken to the caves outside the city walls, where Albert had spent an uncomfortable few hours. Once his first feelings of terror had passed Danglars hoped that they would ask him for money, and let him go. But it soon became clear that he would be there for a long time.

Every time he was hungry and asked for food, the bandits made him pay 100,000 francs. He had now been in the caves for three weeks, and all his money had gone. When he looked at the bandits' hard, unsmiling faces, he thought bitterly, 'They

terror a feeling of great fear

caretaker a person whose job is to look after a building

aren't sorry for me at all! They'll be happy to see me die!'

Just then he saw a man in the shadows at one end of the cave. 'Are you sorry for what you've done?' asked the man.

'Oh yes!' replied Danglars. 'I know I've done wicked things!'

'Then I can give you a pardon,' said the man, stepping forward into the light.

'The Count of Monte Cristo!' cried Danglars.

'You're wrong. I'm the man whose happiness you destroyed, many years ago. I am Edmond Dantès!'

Danglars gave a cry and fell to the ground.

'Get up,' said the count, raising the poor man to his feet. 'You're lucky – one of your friends is mad, and the other is dead. Vampa, give this man his money back, and let him go free.'

'The Count of Monte Cristo!' cried Danglars.

On October 4th, Maximilien arrived on the island of Monte Cristo in the count's boat. The count took him into his underground palace. The young man was impressed, but the count noticed that he never smiled.

'So you are still depressed, my friend?' he asked gently.

'How could you think anything else, Count? I came here to join you in order to die in the arms of a friend.'

'I can help you,' said the count and he gave a teaspoon of something thick and green to Maximilien, who put it in his mouth.

Soon Maximilien felt a terrible pain in his side. 'My friend, I think I'm dying,' he said to the count. 'Thank you for your help.' And with that his eyes closed.

Then a light seemed to shine in his darkness, and a woman was holding his hand and talking lovingly to him.

'Once the sleeping potion stops working he will wake up. And then you must never leave him, Valentine,' said the count. 'I am only sorry that it took me so long to bring you safely out of your sleep of the dead. But from what I have seen of Maximilien this last month, one thing is sure. To be happy in this world or the next, you need each other.'

'Oh, thank you, Count!' whispered Valentine. 'But you must think of your own happiness now. Look who is here!'

The count turned, to see Haydée in the doorway.

'My lord, do you know how much I love you?' she said.

'Haydée, if you were a free woman and not a slave, could you still love me?'

Haydée did not answer, but ran to kiss him, and when Valentine looked again, they had both disappeared.

An hour later Maximilien woke. 'Oh, I'm still alive!' he cried, and he tried to take a knife from the table near him.

'My dear,' said Valentine, smiling, 'here I am.'

He gave a great cry and took her in his arms.

After some time they went to look for the count, and discovered that he and Haydée had already left the island.

'Will we ever see him again?' asked Maximilien sadly.

'My dearest,' replied Valentine, 'we must do what he always did – wait and hope.'

READING CHECK

Are these sentences true or false? Tick the boxes.   True False

a Albert leaves Marseille as a sailor on a cargo ship. ☐ ☑

b Mercedes is living in her father's house in Marseille. ☐ ☐

c The count and Mercedes say goodbye forever. ☐ ☐

d Danglars goes to Rome and gets five million francs there. ☐ ☐

e Luigi Vampa tells Danglars that he is Edmond Dantès. ☐ ☐

f Danglars is sorry for the wicked things that he has done. ☐ ☐

g The count tells Luigi Vampa to let Danglars die. ☐ ☐

h The prison of the Château d'If is open to the public. ☐ ☐

i The count takes Albert to the island of Monte Cristo. ☐ ☐

j Valentine dies on the island. ☐ ☐

k Haydée is in love with the count. ☐ ☐

WORD WORK

Use the words in the crossword to complete the sentences.

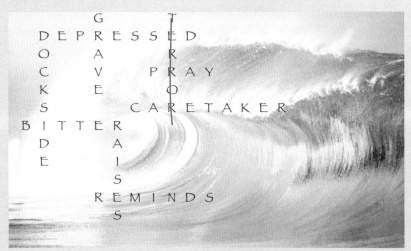

```
        G       T
   D E P R E S S E D
   O   A       R
   C   V     P R A Y
   K   E       O
   S       C A R E T A K E R
 B I T T E R
   D       R
   E       A
           I
           S
   R E M I N D S
           S
```

a The count is filled with ....terror.... when he visits the Château d'If again.

b A .... shows the count his old cell.

c The visit .... him of the horror of his time in prison.

d The count sees Mercedes waving goodbye to Albert on the .... in Marseille.

e Life is .... for Mercedes now that she is alone.

f She says that she will stay in Edmond's father's old house and ....

g The count .... Mercedes' hand to his lips.

h Maximilien feels .... after Valentine's death.

i In Marseille, Maximilien goes to visit his father's ....

GUESS WHAT

1 What happens after the story ends? Choose from these ideas or add your own.

a ☐ Haydée and the count go and live on the island of Monte Cristo.

b ☐ Maximilien and Valentine get married and go back to care for Villefort in Paris.

c ☐ Mercedes dies of a broken heart.

d ☐ Albert dies in North Africa.

e ☐ Albert comes back to Marseille to care for his mother.

f ☐ Luigi Vampa robs Monte Cristo.

g ☐ Baron Danglars joins Luigi Vampa and becomes a bandit.

2 What do you think? Talk about your ideas with a partner.

	Agree	Disagree
a The Count of Monte Cristo was right to get his revenge.	☐	☐
b The count's disguises are interesting.	☐	☐
c Villefort was a very bad person.	☐	☐
d Danglars has no good reason to hate Edmond Dantès.	☐	☐
e Mercedes was wrong to marry Fernand.	☐	☐
f At the end of the story the count was wrong to leave Mercedes.	☐	☐
g Albert de Morcerf must pay for his father's crime.	☐	☐
h The count cannot marry Haydée because she is a slave.	☐	☐
i The count helped Maximilien and Valentine because they have good hearts.	☐	☐
j The count makes friends with bandits because he is naturally wicked.	☐	☐

Project A — *A Book Review*

1 Circle the words to complete the sentences.

a *The Count of Monte Cristo* is   a real   a historical adventure   a ghost   story.

b The story takes place mostly in   Italy   Greece   France .

c It happens during the time of   Napoleon   Joan of Arc   Asterix the Gaul .

d The story is about   Andrea Cavalcanti   Edmond Dantès   Father Faria
getting revenge on Danglars, Fernand, and Villefort for sending him to prison.

e There is another story in the book about the Count of Monte Cristo helping
Albert and Eugénie   Maximilien and Valentine   Valentine and Franz   to marry.

f The main person in the story is   Sinbad the Sailor   Lord Wilmore   Edmond Dantès
who puts on different disguises at different times.

g I thought the book was   dull   difficult to get into   readable   a real page-turner
unputdownable   excellent .

2 Match the words with the definitions. Use a dictionary to help you.

a .... the writer

b .... when a story happens

c .... where a story happens

d .... the most important part
of the story

e .... a less important part of
the story

f .... a person in a story

g .... a long story that fills a
whole book

h .... the kind of story it is
(detective, adventure,
romantic)

character
genre
novel
author
period
plot
setting
subplot

3 **Use words from Activity 2 to complete this review of another novel by Dumas,**
The Three Musketeers.

'The Three Musketeers' is a novel in the historical adventure **(a)**....................

It was written in 1844 by the French **(b)**.................... Alexandre Dumas. The

(c).................... of the novel is in France and England, and the **(d)**....................

is during the time of Louis XV. The main **(e)**.................... in the book is d'Artagnan, a

young man from Gascony, who joins the King's musketeers. Other important characters

are Porthos, Athos and Aramis – the three musketeers who become d'Artagnan's friends.

D'Artagnan's enemy is the wicked Milady. There are historical characters too, like the King

and Queen of France, Richelieu and the Duke of Buckingham. The main **(f)**....................

is about the musketeers helping the Queen to get some diamonds back. There is a

romantic **(g)**.................... about d'Artagnan's love for Constance Bonacieux. I thought it

was a very readable story and once I had started it I couldn't put it down. I feel sure other

readers will enjoy it, too. In short, an excellent book.

4 **Now write a review of** *The Count of Monte Cristo.* **Say what you think about it.**
(Read the back of the book and about Dumas's life at the front to help you.)

Project B *Great Escapes*

1 Read the story of the escape from Alcatraz and complete the note card below.

Escape from Alcatraz

Alcatraz is an island prison which lies two kilometres from San Francisco, California, in very cold and dangerous water. Frank Morris was sent to Alcatraz for robbing banks. Using metal spoons he and three other men, John and Clarence Anglin (also bank robbers) and Allen West (a car thief), had made tunnels from their cells up to the roof of the prison. On June 11th 1962 the Anglin brothers decided to escape and Morris went with them. They had made painted heads which they put at the top of their beds to stop the guards noticing their escape. After climbing onto the roof, Morris and the Anglin brothers climbed down the outside walls of the prison building and jumped into the sea. They entered the water at about ten o'clock that night. They had made 'water wings' from plastic raincoats that they filled with air to help them keep their heads above water in the cold sea. They were never found. Did they escape or did they die in the sea? Nobody knows. West was too late leaving his cell and stayed in prison for the rest of his life.

Name of prisoners

Why were they in prison?

Name of prison

Where was the prison?

Date of escape

How did the prisoners leave their cells?

How did the prisoners leave the prison?

How did they stop the guards noticing their escape?

Did all the prisoners escape?

2 Use the information in the note cards to complete the story on page 76 of the escape from Donington Hall.

Name of prisoners *Gunter Plüschow and Oberleutnant Trefftz*

Why were they in prison? *German prisoners of war in First World War*

Name of prison *Donington Hall*

Where was the prison? *near Derby, England*

Date of escape *July 4th 1915*

How did the prisoners leave the prison? *In the afternoon, went into park where prisoners could go walking during day, and hid among some garden chairs when guards and other prisoners went back inside prison. That evening at midnight, came out of hiding place and climbed over thick wire fence. They walked to Derby, where caught different trains to London.*

How did they stop the guards noticing their escape? *Friends lay in their beds that evening to make guards think that they were ill in bed.*

Did both prisoners escape? *Trefftz was caught on way to London.*

Did Plüschow use a false identity? *Called himself George Mine, a British dockside worker; he made his elegant clothes dirty and darkened his fair hair with black shoe polish.*

Where did he escape to? *Got onto a Dutch boat in London and sailed to Amsterdam, where he was safe.*

75

Escape from Donington Hall

.... and ....
.... were .... prisoners
of .... They were sent to ....
.... They escaped on
.... That afternoon ....
.... Later that evening ....
.... There they caught ....
....

That night friends ....
On the way to London ....
but Plüschow escaped. He called himself .... and
.... In this way he got ....
....

3   Complete the note card about the escape from the Château d'If in Chapters 3 and 4 of this book.

Name of prisoner
Name of prison
Date of escape
How did the prisoner leave his cell?
How did he leave the prison?
What did he do to stop the guards noticing his escape?
Did he use a false identity?
Where did he escape to?

4   Write the story of Dantès' escape from prison. Use the note card in Activity 3 and the stories on pages 74–75 to help you.

GRAMMAR CHECK

Reported requests and commands

We use *ask* + *(not)* *to* + *infinitive* for reported requests.

'Please join me here for lunch,' said the count to Franz and Albert.

The count asked Franz and Albert to join him there for lunch.

We use *tell* + *(not)* *to* + *infinitive* for reported commands.

'Don't worry about Albert,' the count said to Franz.

The count told Franz not to worry about Albert.

In reported requests and commands, we change personal pronouns to match the speaker and the situation. Also, *here* becomes *there*, and *come* becomes *go*.

1 Write the sentences again. Use reported requests and commands.

a 'Please think about our wedding, Mercedes,' Fernand said.
   Fernand asked Mercedes to think about their wedding.

b 'Don't ask me about that any more, Fernand,' said Mercedes.
   ....

c 'Shake hands with Edmond like a friend,' she said to Fernand.
   ....

d 'Write a short letter to Villefort,' Danglars said to Fernand.
   ....

e 'Please get me out of here!' Edmond said to the prison inspector.
   ....

f 'Please come and visit me in my cell,' the priest said to Edmond.
   ....

g 'Take the treasure and use it for yourself, Edmond,' said the priest.
   ....

h 'Set the young man free,' Luigi Vampa said to his men.
   ....

GRAMMAR CHECK

Present Simple passive and Past Simple passive

We use the passive when we are interested in a situation or an action, rather than in the person who does the action.

Edmond is kept in prison for a long time. (= we don't know who keeps him there.)

We make the Present Simple passive with am/is/are + past participle form of the verb.

Haydée is sold as a slave.   *Morrel's debts are all paid.*

We make the Past Simple passive with was/were + past participle form of the verb.

In 1815, Napoleon was banished to the island of Saint Helena.

2 Complete the text. Use the Present Simple passive or the Past Simple passive form of the verbs in brackets.

My dearest Mercedes,

I don't know if you will ever read this letter. When I a) **was arrested** (arrest) two days ago, I b) .... (take) to see Villefort, the crown prosecutor, and I c) .... (ask) to hand over the letter that I was carrrying. I think that the envelope d) .... (address) to Villefort's father. Villefort made sure that the letter e) .... (destroy), and I thought I would soon be free. But I f) .... (keep) at the police station for several hours, and then I g) .... (put) in a boat and I h) .... (row) out to the Château d'If - you know, where all the dangerous criminals i) .... (lock up)!

Now I j) .... (shut) in a cell here! I know that nobody k) .... (let out) of this prison. It's dark and cold, and I l) .... (give) only dry bread to eat every day. I m) .... (watch) carefully by the guards, to stop me escaping. Maybe I'll never see you again!

Your ever-loving Edmond

GRAMMAR CHECK

Modal auxiliary verbs: must, may, and can't

We use *must* + *be* when we think that something is true.

That must be Morrel's ship sailing in. I recognize its sails!

We use *may* + *be* when we think that there is a possibility that something is true, but we are not sure.

Fernand may be a friend of Edmond's, but I don't think he is.

We use *can't* + *be* when we think that something is not true.

This letter can't be for Monsieur Villefort. The address at the front is not his!

3 Complete Edmond's thoughts in the story. Use *must*, *may*, or *can't*.

a This ..*can't*.. be right! I haven't committed any crime!

b I .... be in prison for just a few days, or perhaps a little longer.

c I can hear a noise in the wall. It .... be another prisoner. I'm sure it is.

d The guards .... be here yet, so I still have time to get into Father Faria's sack.

e They're throwing me into the sea! This .... be what they call the graveyard of the Château d'If!

f The men on that ship .... be smugglers, but I'm not sure.

g Mercedes .... be married by now, but I don't know if she is.

h My enemies .... be Danglars, Fernand, and Villefort. I know that they were the people who put me in prison.

i This .... be the right place for the caves. I haven't reached the twentieth rock yet.

j Look at all that treasure! There .... be enough here to make me one of the richest men in the world!

GRAMMAR CHECK

Gerund with sense verbs

The gerund (–ing form) is the noun form of a verb. To make the gerund, we usually add –ing to the verb, but when a verb ends in consonant + –e, we remove the e and add –ing.

sail – sailing   ride – riding

We use the gerund after sense verbs – such as see, watch, hear, listen, and feel – to show that the action we are observing or experiencing is continuing.

I saw Napoleon giving Edmond a letter.

Somebody heard Danglars making a plan with Fernand.

Edmond didn't want anybody to watch him finding the treasure.

Lord Wilmore listened to Monsieur Boville talking about Morrel's debts.

Maximilien drank the count's medicine and felt himself dying.

4 Complete the sentences. Use the *–ing* form of the verbs in the box.

look	talk	shake	have	tell
shudder	laugh	ask	make	~~enter~~

a Albert and his friends watched the count ..entering.. the room.

b They all saw the count .... hands with Maximilien.

c The count heard Debray .... at the idea of Albert being in danger.

d Albert's friends listened to him .... the story of his kidnap.

e The count saw them .... at him with great interest.

f The count heard Albert .... about Baron Danglars.

g For a while, the count listened to the young men .... conversation.

h Fernand did not see the count .... lunch with Albert and his friends.

i Mercedes did not hear the count .... Albert who he was planning to marry.

j Albert saw his mother .... and thought she was ill.

GRAMMAR CHECK

Suffixes: –ly, –ily, –en, –ful, –ed, –d, –er, and –or

We can add the suffixes –ly or –ily to an adjective to make some adverbs.

Morrel's daughter speaks gratefully to the count.

Edmond looks dreamily at the gold and jewels in his hands. (dreamy –y + ily)

We can add the suffix –en to an adjective to make some verbs.

The sky darkened as the sailors watched.   *Waiting maddened them.*

We can add the suffixes –ful, –ed, and –d to a verb or noun to make some adjectives.

Lord Wilmore is very helpful to the Morrel family.

Edmond is delighted when he finds the treasure.

He is excited at the thought of escaping.

We can add the suffixes –or or –er to a verb or noun to make words for people.

Villefort, the crown prosecutor, tells the police officers to take Edmond away.

5 Complete the text. Use the words in brackets with the suffixes in the box. You must use some suffixes more than once and make some spelling changes.

–ily	–ful	–en	–ly	–er	–d	–ed

Soon after Fernand arrived in the Upper House, he realized that everybody was looking

a) ...*angrily*... (angry) at him. He was asked to say b) ....
(honest) whether he had had anything to do with Ali Pasha's murder.
He stood up c) .... (slow). He was d) .... (hope) that
he could lie to them e) .... (confident). But f) ....
(sudden) a g) .... (beauty) girl spoke from the public seats.
Everyone turned to look at her, h) .... (surprise).
'Traitor!' she cried i) .... (loud) and j) .... (excited).
'You took the enemy's gold and helped them k) .... (cruel)
to kill my father, Ali Pasha! You're a l) .... (murder)! You
m) .... (short) his life and n) .... (sad) his family
for ever!' Fernand said nothing. He felt ashamed and he left the
House o) .... (unhappy) because he knew that she was
telling the truth.

GRAMMAR CHECK

Present Perfect Continuous and Past Simple

We use the Present Perfect Continuous to show that a past action or activity is still continuing. To make the Present Perfect Continuous, we use the has/have + been + –ing verb form.

'Edmond *has been visiting* Mercedes,' Fernand said angrily.

'I've *been expecting* you!' Edmond told the prison inspector.

We use the Past Simple to talk about actions that are finished. We often use the Past Simple with time expressions such as yesterday, last week, and a few months ago.

Madame Danglars *saw* the count's new horses yesterday.

The count *saved* Albert from the bandits several days ago.

6 Complete the text. Use the Present Perfect Continuous or Past Simple form of the verbs in brackets.

I can't believe it – my dear Valentine is dead! I
a) ...have been worrying... (worry) about her for weeks
now. All the time, she b) .... (get) thinner and thinner
and she c) .... (look) paler and paler. All these years,
I d) .... (wait) to marry her. All this time, I
e) .... (hope) to make her my wife one day.

Her stepmother f) .... (try) to poison her for some time.
Yesterday, the wicked woman g) .... (succeed)! Poor
Valentine h) .... (die) in her sleep. Several weeks ago,
the count i) .... (promise) me that he would look after
Valentine, but I suppose that, recently, he j) .... (think)
of other things. All today, the women servants k) ....
(prepare) Valentine's body – and now she's in her coffin. It's too
horrible to think of! I know that they l) .... (pray) for
her all day, too. I can still hear their prayers.

My life's worth nothing now. In fact, I m) ....
(wonder) whether to put an end to it all – I'm still thinking
about it.

GRAMMAR CHECK

Past Perfect: affirmative

We use the Past Perfect when we are already talking about the past (using the Past Simple) and we want to talk about an action that happened earlier in the past, before the Past Simple action. To make the Past Perfect, we use had + past participle.

By the time he escaped, Edmond had been in prison for fourteen years.

We often use when + Past Simple in a sentence containing the Past Perfect.

Mercedes had lost all hope of seeing Edmond again when she married Fernand.

We often use time expressions – such as **by that time**, **already**, and **by then** – with the Past Perfect.

7 Complete the sentences. Use the Past Perfect or Past Simple form of the verbs in brackets.

a Valentine's grandfather
  .made. (make) it clear that he
  .had murdered. (murder)
  Franz's father in 1815.

b Albert .... (find out) that his
  father .... (accept) money
  from the enemy.

c It was clear that Andrea Cavalcanti .... (commit) a murder some time
  before when the police at last .... (arrest) him.

d People .... (go) to look for Eugénie Danglars, but by then, she ....
  (left) to travel round Europe with a friend.

e Fernand .... (shoot) himself because everybody .... (realize) by
  that time that he was a traitor.

f When Maximilien .... (hear) that Valentine .... (die), he
  .... (think) that his life .... (end).

g The Count of Monte Cristo .... (begin) to think that he ....
  (already/have) his revenge.

DOMINOES THE STRUCTURED APPROACH TO READING IN ENGLISH

Dominoes is an enjoyable series of illustrated classic and modern stories in four carefully graded language stages – from Starter to Three – which take learners from beginner to intermediate level.

Each *Domino* reader includes:
- a **good story** to read and enjoy
- **integrated activities** to develop reading skills and increase active vocabulary
- **personalized projects** to make the language and story themes more meaningful
- **seven pages of grammar activities** for consolidation.

Each *Domino* pack contains a reader, plus a MultiROM with:
- a **complete audio recording of the story**, fully dramatized to bring it to life
- **interactive activities** to offer further practice in reading and language skills and to consolidate learning.

If you liked this Level Three *Domino*, why not read these?

The Moonstone
Wilkie Collins

The Moonstone is a beautiful yellow diamond that was stolen from the statue of a Moon god in India. When Franklin Blake brings it to Rachel Verinder's house in Yorkshire for her birthday, it brings bad luck with it. How many people will the Moonstone hurt? How many must die before the diamond's revenge is complete?

Book ISBN: 978 0 19 424821 1
MultiROM Pack ISBN: 978 0 19 424779 5

Mansfield Park
Jane Austen

'Why shouldn't we offer to take care of her? She could live with us at Mansfield.'

In this way Mrs Norris persuades her sister, Lady Bertram, and Lady Bertram's husband, Sir Thomas, to ask their poor niece Fanny Price to live with them at Mansfield Park.

At first Fanny is unhappy there. Then, after she makes friends with her young cousins, things improve. But what happens when the cousins are older, and starting to think of love?

Book ISBN: 978 0 19 424828 0
MultiROM Pack ISBN: 978 0 19 424786 3

You can find details and a full list of books in the *Dominoes* catalogue and Oxford English Language Teaching Catalogue, and on the website: www.oup.com/elt

Teachers: see www.oup.com/elt for a full range of online support, or consult your local office.

	CEFR	Cambridge Exams	IELTS	TOEFL iBT	TOEIC
Level 3	B1	PET	4.0	57-86	550
Level 2	A2–B1	KET-PET	3.0-4.0	–	–
Level 1	A1–A2	YLE Flyers/KET	3.0	–	–
Starter & Quick Starter	A1	YLE Movers	–	–	–